Book of D

An anthology of creative writing by the children
of Boughton Monchelsea Primary School

This book has been edited and published by Boughton Monchelsea PTA
Committee to raise money for the school. We are particularly grateful to
Alison Hodges, whose idea this was. A huge thank you to all the children
for producing such lovely writing and artwork. Thank you, too, to all the
staff – Jerry Jarvis, Sally Christmas, Peter Hirons, Magi Swann, Jenny
Godden, Lucy Thomas, Sharon Taylor, Charlotte Ball, and Jean Rogers –
without whose support this book would not have been possible.

CONTENTS BY THE CHILDREN OF
Boughton Monchelsea Primary School

First published 2005

Published by TheSchoolBook.com
www.theschoolbook.com
t: (+44) 01284 700321

ISBN: 1-84549-028-2

Printed and bound in the United Kingdom

Typeset in Garamond 10/12/14/16/20

TheSchoolBook.com is an imprint of arima
publishing
The ASK Building, Northgate Avenue
Bury St Edmunds, Suffolk IP32 6BB
www.arimapublishing.com

CHAPTER 1

CHAPTER 2

CHAPTER 3

CHAPTER 1

Reception Class Dreams

Jacob Carter

The Monster

In my best dream a monster came into my house. The monster ate our food and sat on the table and the house. The monster was bigger than the house. The monster was called Jack and he was green with grey eyes.

Thomas Carter

Playing with Harry Potter

My favourite dream is about Harry Potter. We had rocket boots so we could fly. We went to my friend Max's house and played Spiderman. Then Harry Potter had to go home.

Shirin Deboo

Dogs and a Cat

My best dream was when my dogs kissed me. Max ran around
the coffee table and barked at the window. I opened the door
and a cat came in. The cat had a fight with the dog and the dog
ran outside. Tom had to chase the dog and Rachel gave the dog a
treat.

Tommy Doherty

The Dolphin

In my dream a dolphin kissed me. He wanted to come home with
me and have dinner with me. He wanted me to come to his
house. We went for a swim and had a sleepover with the dolphin.

Joel Faulkner

Boy Racer

I like to dream about being a racer. In my dream I win all the
races. Thomas comes second and Leo comes third. I win the cup!
I go and celebrate with my friends and then go home. When I go
home I go to bed straight away.

Max Freeman

The Spaceman

I like to dream about being a spaceman. I look at all the planets
in my rocket. Thomas is a spaceman too. In my dream we land
on planets to check what they look like.

Christine Gander

The Unicorn

My best dream is about a unicorn. The butterfly came to see the
unicorn who was on its own in a dark wood. They looked up and
they saw another unicorn flying with wings. They wanted to fly
too. The unicorn with wings taught them to fly.

Grace Goodwin

The Princess Dream

I dreamed about a princess. She had a castle and there was a
queen and king. The princess and the king danced together and
had dinner.

Alicia Grassom

Princesses

My favourite dreams are about princesses. I dream about meeting princesses in Disneyland. I play with the princesses and we go swimming. We go on the swings and sometimes sing together.

Jade Hall

Cinderella

I dreamed about Cinderella. She lived with the king and queen and a dragon. The dragon ate her and the king and queen were sad. Cinderella came back to life and married the prince.

Ellie Hastings-Strike

Snails and Butterflies

In my dream the snail's shell fell off. Then the caterpillar turned
into a butterfly. I picked up the butterfly and let him fly away.
Then I woke up.

Leo Hodges

Going to the Fair

I like to dream about going to the fair. There is knife throwing
and dancing. There were cowboys and I ate a burger. At the end
of the dream I got wet because the cowboys put water on our
heads.

Charlie Horne

Friends with Spiderman

In my dream Spiderman saves me from the doctor. I make friends with Spiderman and turn into Spiderman. I climb up the walls and get the doctor. Then I go to work and take some photos of Spiderman.

Josie Jackson

The Tooth Fairy

In my dream a fairy was flying around my house. The fairy picked up my tooth. The fairy put the tooth somewhere safe and put a shiny coin under my pillow.

Bryony Jenner

Disneyland

I like to dream about Disneyland. I talked to Minnie Mouse and Cinderella. Me and Harriet watched the parade and had an ice-cream.

Hannah Johnson

Picnic with a Princess

In my favourite dream I play with my little sister. We play in the garden on the swing. A princess comes to have a picnic with us and we play together.

Eliska Jolliffe

Lizards in the Bed

I dream about lizards. They sleep in my bed and Daddy puts them in the garden. Me and my brother Michael play in the garden in my dream. We play with the dog and the dog eats the grass.

Jason Leith

Tank Battle

In my dream the tanks had a battle. I had a tank ride and destroyed the other team. There was an army with soldiers and a house fell down. The army was surrounded and the soldiers were fighting and shooting. The T-Rex chased the soldiers.

Megan Lindsay

Cousins

I dreamed about horse riding. I saw my cousins in the dream. My cousins walked with a pony in a circus. My cousins' names are Ruby and Elizabeth and they both have blue eyes. Me and Jacob laughed at the clowns in the circus. Jacob fell asleep.

Abby Mackay

Flowers and Parties

I like to dream about planting some flowers in my garden and outside the front door. I like to dream about my party when I played with my friends. We played games and had party food.

Georgia Mehmet-Bussey

The Friendly Monster

I like to dream about a friendly monster. The monster cooked some toast for me and he was friendly to me and Mummy. The monster played with me and looked after me. The monster gave me a pink and purple butterfly.

Euan Mitchell

Shopkeeper

My favourite dream is about going to Daddy's shop. I sell things to the customers with my Daddy. I eat the sweets in the shop and have fun.

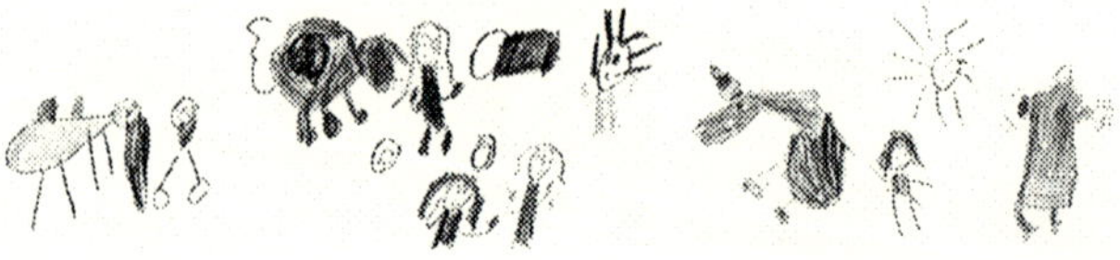

Tom Pearson

In a Spaceship

My favourite dream is when I dream I'm in a spaceship. The spaceship turns into a plane and a horse and it goes really fast. It takes me swimming and to Legoland and it's really cool!

Phoebe Simpson

Lunch with Mickey Mouse

My favourite dream is about Disneyland. I saw the parade and Tinkerbell. I played with Minnie and we went on some rides. I had lunch with Mickey Mouse.

Amber Slater

Disney Holiday

I love dreaming about holidays. Mummy and Daddy come too. We went on a Winnie The Pooh ride and Peter Pan ride. I met Mickey Mouse. In my dream I went for a swim.

Harry Spice

Seaside Holidays

My favourite dream is about holidays to the seaside. I dream about collecting shells and stones. Me and Megan look at fish and we have a picnic. I played in the sand with Charlie. It was quite fun.

Madison Waters

Princesses with Butterflies

My favourite dream is when I dream of princesses holding butterflies on their hands. Belle the princess sings and I dance on the stage with her. We both sing songs then we both go to McDonald's.

Sophie Whitfield

The Picnic

I dreamed that I went for a picnic with Thomas. It was a sunny day and we ate toast and butter. We saw an ant and drank coke.

The Boat and the Dolphin

I like to dream about being in a boat and jumping into the sea. I would like to find a deep bit and make friends with a dolphin. Mummy, Daddy, Rosy, Nanny and Grandad and my Aunty would be on the boat too. I would make the dolphin speak to Mummy and I would swim with the dolphin.

CHAPTER 2

Dreams of Class 1

Lauren Bennett

To be a Princess

I dreamt that I was a princess so that I could live in a beautiful castle.

Rebecca Bishop

Swimming with a Dolphin

When I go to sleep I dream of swimming with a dolphin with me riding on its back. We will swim in and out of the waves.

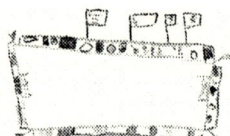

James Blacknell

Fantastic Footballer

My dream is to be a fantastic footballer like David Beckham and I will score 100 goals. I want to play for Chelsea and I want to play for England, and after playing for Chelsea I want to play for Manchester United.

Ben Butcher

Shopping

My dream is going to London and to go shopping and buy a racing car. My racing car would be red and after I buy it I race it home.

William Campbell

Being a Croc

I dream about being a crocodile. I would eat up people and I would also eat up dolphins. My body would be green and my teeth would be very sharp.

Phoebe Cox

Ballerina

I dreamed about being a ballerina. I like it when people smile at me while I am dancing. I would wear a ballerina outfit.

Mollie Cross

Being a Dolphin

My dream was being a dolphin and then I can jump out of the water. I can swim with the fish. I will fight the sharks then the people will be safe and I can carry on with the fish.

Ryan Golding

One Dark Night

One dark night I dreamed about being a footballer. I was Kesman and Chelsea won the cup. After we won I ran around the pitch with my shirt on my head.

Abraham Hicks

I Wish

I wish that I could climb walls like Spiderman. I would wear an outfit like Spiderman too.

Alex Hodges

Fire

In my dream there was a burning house. I would put the fire out with water from my hose. I would arrive in my big red fire engine.

Kerenza Keddy

Sparkling Singer

I want to be a singer when I grow up because I would like to sing spinning around. Another thing I could wear a sparkly t-shirt and skirt. I would sing on a stage and my Mum and Dad would watch me.

Georgina King

Being Chased

One night I had a dream and a ghost was chasing me and I found myself in a jungle.

Fraser Lee

On Track

I would like to be a famous racing car driver.

Jack Lee

Penalty

I wish I could be a fantastic football player. I would score a penalty and after all my team will cheer.

William Lucette

Dream Job

My dream is to be a fireman. I would put lots of fires out and help people get out of buildings. If there was a fire at school I would put it out with a hose.

Taylor Poad

The Stage

I go in my bed to go to sleep, I dream about a stage with me singing and dancing and everybody clapping.

Morgan Potter

Goals

I wish I was a footballer and I would score five goals. I would play for Arsenal and we would win.

Trudi Proctor

Being a Princess

Sometimes I dream I am a princess in a castle. The handsome prince came to the castle and threw a stone. The prince tried to wake me up because he wanted me to climb down the pipe on the tower.

Owen Rixon

To be King

My dream is I was a king. I would live in a castle. I would ride around on a brown horse and his name would be Harry.

Emma Rogers

The Handsome Prince

I want to be a princess when I grow up because I could wear a pretty dress and dance with the handsome prince. I would also wear a cloak and I could live in a castle with lots of rooms.

Georgia Rogers

A Swimmer

I dream about being a swimmer. I like swimming with my dragon. He has ropes on him so I don't fall off.

Joshua Skinner

Snowboarder

If I was a snowboarder I would be the best. My snowboard would be red and my outfit would also be red. I would always wear a helmet and eye goggles.

Letitia Smith

Pop Star

My dream was about a pop star and I won a medal because I was the best. Another thing I sang a song. I would sing on a stage very loudly and I would sing 5, 6, 7, 8.

Phoebe Smith

Beautiful Pictures

I dreamed about being a fantastic artist. I would paint beautiful pictures. My paintings would hang on my wall in my bedroom. I would paint pictures of Bratz dolls.

Ryan Smith

Flying

If I was in an aeroplane I would fly to sunny Barbados.

Abigail Thirkell

The Vet

I dreamt that I would be a vet and if I was a vet I would do an operation on the dog called Sam. The dog would be much better after the operation.

Ross Thompson

The Outing

I dreamed of going to the dinosaur museum because it sounded good. After that we bought an ice-cream. Then we went where moving dinosaurs were, then we found a sea dinosaur.

Samuel Thorpe

Snowboarder

My dream is to be a snowboarder. I will do lots of tricks. I would do lots of flips and land on the white, soft snow.

Caitlin Till

I Wish...

I lived in a beautiful castle and wore a beautiful dress. There is a unicorn that lives next to the castle that always keeps me safe.

Conor Tomkin

Yellow Card

If I was a footballer I would score a goal. Afterwards when my team mates score a goal I cheer but I am sad when one of my team mates gets a yellow card.

CHAPTER 3

Class 2 Dreams

Jessica Bennett

Dreams can be...

Dreams can be big humungous vast gigantic
Dreams can be scary frightening spooky.
Dreams can be crazy loopy bonkers bananas!

Oliver Butters

Dinosaur

I dreamed I was a dinosaur wrecking the enormous city. I had big
spikes on my back and had gigantic claws.

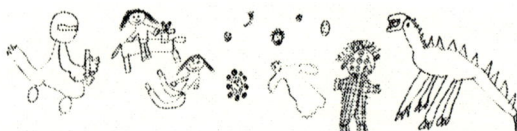

James Campbell

Motorbike Riding

I dreamed I was a famous motorbike rider and I had a shiny helmet. A new player passed me but I zoomed on and won the race.

Edward Clark

Cool Dude

I dreamed I was a motorbike rider and I looked like a cool dude.

Max Davidson

Dreams can be...

Dreams can be silly crazy bananas.
Dreams can be fast supersonic dashy speedy.
Dreams can be frightening scary dark lonely spooky ghostly.

Christian Fletcher

Dreams can be …

Dreams can be scary spooky ghostly terrifying.
Dreams can be fast supersonic speedy quick.
Dreams can be happy cool funny exciting.

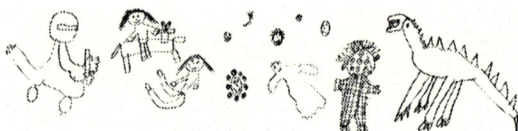

Jack French

Dreams can be...

Dreams can be scary nightmarish terrifying spooky.
Dreams can be big vast massive huge gigantic.
Dreams can be happy joyful cheerful giggly.

Philippa Golding

Magic Tricks

I dreamed I was a famous magician with extremely good tricks. I
had a round of applause and the children laughed and their backs
went on the floor and their legs went in the air.

Emilie Guilfoyle

Dreams can be...

Dreams can be fantastic cool lovely.
Dreams can be big huge vast colossal enormous gigantic.
Dreams can be silly crazy bonkers crackers!
Dreams can be scary spooky ghostly terrifying.

Elliot Harwood

The Fair

I dreamed I was at the fair. I had lots of candy floss.

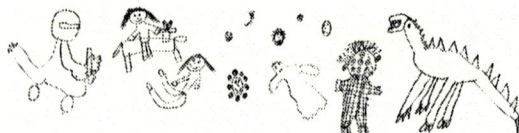

Ryan Harwood

The Soldier

I dreamed I was a soldier. I fought all the baddies and luckily I found James Bond and we won the battle.

George Hill

The Tiger

I dreamed I was a tiger and I roared and roared. Mummy tiger was asleep so I kept roaring. Mummy tiger woke up and yawned.

Charlotte Holgate

Dreams can be...

Dreams can be scary frightening spooky shivery wicked
frightful shocking.
Dreams can be happy joyful funny exciting.
Dreams can be silly crazy bonkers mad!

Billie Holland

A Cat

I dreamed I was a purring cat, miaowing all the time. One day I
lost my voice and then I never purred again. Then a few days
after that I lost my appetite for mouse stew - but I started to eat
ice-cream!

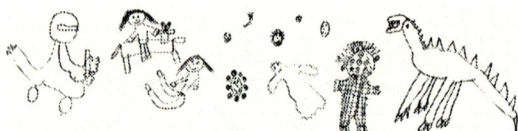

Laura Howard

Zooming Swimmer

I dreamed I was a zooming swimmer with a Mickey Mouse
swimsuit. I splashed a lot and splashed my teacher.

Max Hyde

Dreams can be...

Dreams can be silly dopy crazy.
Dreams can be big vast.
Dreams can be scary spooky creepy.

Chloe Ikin

Dreams can be...

Dreams can be happy great exciting cheerful
Dreams can be sad cheerless upsetting.
Dreams can be silly crazy bonkers!

Harriet Jenner

Fairy Friends

I dreamed I saw a fairy, she told me about her fairy friends. She
had a lovely cottage. She gave me a bed. It was exciting in fairy
world, it was better than my house. It was better than anything.

Charlotte Johnstone

Dreams can be...

Dreams can be scary spooky frightening.
Dreams can be happy joyful cheerful.
Dreams can be sad upsetting cheerless unhappy.
Dreams can be annoying ferocious fuming.
Dreams can be silly stupid bonkers.

Ben Jones

Lizard

I dreamed I was a lizard. When enemies were after me I left my tail behind. After two weeks I grew a new one. I camouflaged myself in the trees.

Angus Knowler

Driver

I dreamed I was a go-kart driver and had a helmet of silver and blue.

Max Ladbrook

Dreams can be...

Dreams can be fast speedy supersonic.
Dreams can be happy cool amazing.
Dreams can be scary spooky haunted.

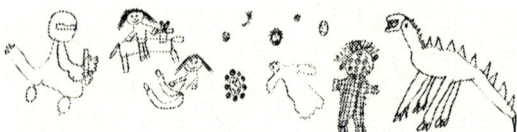

Katherine Luckhurst

Dreams can be...

Dreams can be happy great brilliant joyful funny
magical fantastic.
Dreams can be scary frightful frightening wicked spooky
shivery shocking.
Dreams can be mad annoying crazy bonkers nuts!

Haydn Potter

Dreams can be...

Dreams can be bonkers crazy.
Dreams can be big colossal vast gigantic.
Dreams can be teeny titchy.

Kayleigh Proctor

The Long-haired Fairy

I dreamed I was a tooth fairy with golden hair down to the floor.
I collected a tooth, the floor went creak, and I flew away into the
night.

Megan Spice

Dreams can be...

Dreams can be small tiny little short.
Dreams can be silly bonkers crazy stupid.
Dreams can be happy cheerful jolly pleasant.
Dreams can be sad terrible unhappy cheerless.
Dreams can be big huge vast colossal humungous.

Jack Thatcher

Dreams can be...

Dreams can be silly bonkers mad.
Dreams can be sad broken-hearted upsetting.
Dreams can be happy exciting giggly.

James Thorn

The Hero

I dreamed I was a famous karate teacher and I crushed all the bad people. I had golden clothes and I was a hero.

Gemma Whitfield

Dreams can be...

Dreams can be teeny weeny wincy small.
Dreams can be crazy bonkers mad daft silly stupid.
Dreams can be big humungous gigantic huge!

Francis Wise

Racing Cars

I dreamed I was a famous racing car driver. I noticed I had
knocked a racing car off the track, then the racing car exploded.

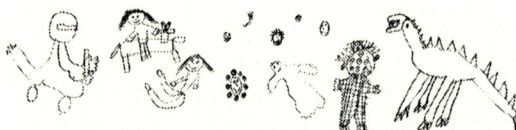

CHAPTER 4

Dreams of Class 3

Megan Bennett

Playgroup

Fast asleep in my bunk bed
I dream of working in a playgroup.
Snuggled soft in a snuggly sleeping bag,
Pictures of pretty children
Like tiny ants.
Dancing they go from toy to toy,
Twirling they dig in the sand.
I feel like a small child
When I dream of playgroup.

Charlotte Bishop

Leaping Frogs

Fast asleep dreaming dreams,
I dream of little leaping frogs in my head.
Snuggled soft in my squashy bed
Pictures of little frogs, big frogs, leaping from lily pad
                                        to lily pad
Like jumping on trampolines.
Dancing they turn round and round,
Twirling they dance under the water.
I feel experienced with the frogs
When I dream of little leaping frogs.

Chelsea Player

Fast asleep in my cosy bed
I dream of famous footballers.
Snuggled soft in my lovely bed
Pictures of me scoring for Chelsea
Like Frank Lampard.
Dancing they kick the ball from player to player
Twirling they jump up and down.
I feel fantastic
When I dream of me in Chelsea.

Amy Coster

When I Grow Up

I was at my house and I had a fabulous dream about being a pop star. I would wear a fancy top and a fancy skirt. I would dance and sing! I would do over fourteen songs! I would do my concerts at Mote Park. At my concert my assistant served drinks, hot dogs and snacks. If only this could come true! I would feel phenomenal!

Molly Crosby

My Future in the Past

When I grow up I want to be an archaeologist because I am interested in history, but you have to be talented to be an archaeologist. You need to be good at science and good at history as well, and if you are good at all these things you can be an archaeologist.

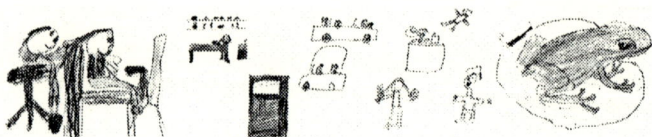

Nathan Cross

Scoring Goals

Fast asleep in my bunk bed
I dream of football.
Snuggled soft in my covers
Pictures of me scoring goals
Like the best footballer.
Dancing they passed the ball from player to player.
Twirling they kicked the ball in the goal and scored.
I feel incredible!
When I dream of me playing for Arsenal.

Pagan Davis

The Artist

Fast asleep in my hot bed
I dream of working as an artist.
Snuggled soft in my Mum and Dad's bed
Pictures of me painting people.
Like beautiful ladies picking roses,
Dancing they wear pink ballerina slippers,
Twirling they kick their heels.
I feel happy
When I dream of working as an artist.

April Drew

The Pterodactyl

Me and my cousins were walking to the shop. We turned around
and saw a pterodactyl. It was huge! We ran as fast as we could!
The pterodactyl was not going to give up until we gave up. My
cousins got eaten right up. But I did not. I kept on going. I
ducked under a very low tree. The pterodactyl bashed into the
tree. That was the end of him.

Matthew Edwards

Like Dennis Bergkamp

Fast asleep in my bunk bed
I dream of being a famous footballer.
Snuggled soft in my dream
Pictures of me scoring goals
Like Dennis Bergkamp.
Dancing they move around the pitch,
Twirling they move around my head.
I feel incredible
When I dream of a famous footballer.

Alice Emmerson

Helping People

When I grow up I will want to be a dentist because I can help
people by looking after their teeth.

The Champions

Fast asleep in my comfy bed,
I dream of playing for Liverpool.
Snuggled soft in my duvet,
Pictures of scoring a phenomenal goal.
Like winning the Champions League.
Dancing they say yeeeees! Liverpool win the Champions League!
Twirling they lift the cup.
I feel incredible!
When I dream of Liverpool winning the Champions League.

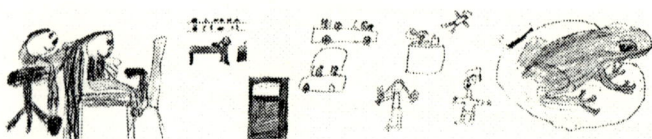

Poppy Freeman

Horseracing

Fast asleep in my cosy bed
I dream of horseracing.
Snuggled soft in my covers
Pictures of incredible horses
Like brown shadows running around.
Dancing they gallop around the field
Twirling they go up and down the field.
I feel fascinated
When I dream of horseracing.

James Gander

Rome

I was a Roman and I was attacking a city. Suddenly a man attacked me. I beat him and another fierce man was going to kill me. It was awful but one of my men with great courage ran in front of me and he bravely defended me. Finally we won the battle. It was hot and I was exhausted. I woke up and found it was a dream.

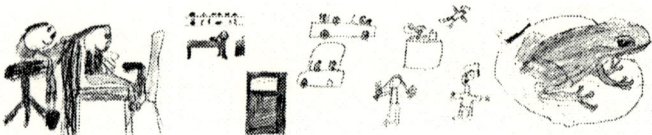

Jemimah Hicks

My Horse

When I grow up I want to be a horse rider and have a lovely horse. Before I ride it I will give it a groom. After that I will ride it around a track then I will find one apple and a carrot and carefully give it to my lovely horse. Whenever I go to have a race I will be wishing to win and if I do win I will put the medal around my horse's neck. I wish to be a horse rider with a lovely horse!

Will Hodges

The job for me

On Monday I wanted to be an agent.
On Tuesday I wanted to be a teacher.
On Wednesday I wanted to be a pilot.
On Thursday I wanted to be an archaeologist.
On Friday I wanted to be an actor.
On Saturday I wanted to be a footballer.
On Sunday I wanted to be a waiter in Pizza Express.

Lottie Holland

The Horse Racer

Fast asleep in my snug-as-a-bug bed
I dream of being a famous horse racer.
Snuggled soft in my bunk bed
Pictures of me riding a horse
Like Penny Pucker.
Dancing they lift their feet up
Twirling they run around before they start the race.
I feel exquisite
When I dream of being a famous horse racer.

Purdy Hood

The Cartoonist

When I grow up I want to be a cartoonist because I am excellent at art. But I think I will have to go to Art School.

Thomas Jackson

Speed Demon

Fast asleep in my gorgeous bunk bed
I dream of a really fast Ferrari.
Snuggled soft in my duvet
Pictures of me going 90mph down the motorway in

my Ferrari

Like a cheetah running through the forest.
Dancing it moves in and out overtaking other cars,
Twirling it skids around the roundabout.
I feel excited in my Ferrari
When I dream of driving in a fast Ferrari.

Ellie Jones

To Be a Vet

When I grow up I want to be a vet because I want to look after animals, but I only want to look after domestic animals. To be a vet I will have to go to university, then I will have to do five or seven years of training. The reason why I want to be a vet is so I can give injections and do operations.

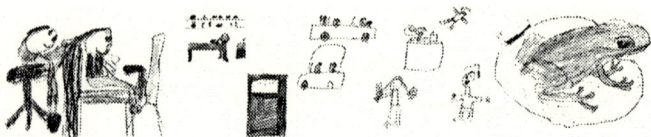

Louis Kemp

Cats

Fast asleep in my bunk bed
I dream of hundreds of cats.
Snuggled soft in my dream
Pictures of cats
Like black wool.
Dancing they dance to and fro.
Twirling they run after me.
I feel happy
When I dream of hundreds of cats.

Joseph Kilbride

My Dog Billy

Fast asleep in my cosy bed
I dream of Billy my dog.
Snuggled soft in a cloud
Pictures of hot air balloons
Like white fluffy clouds.
Dancing he jumps up and down on the clouds,
Twirling he turns side to side.
I feel the soft cloud
When I dream of my dream.

Matthew Mansell

Shoot and Score

Fast asleep in my snuggly bed
I dream of being an Arsenal player.
Snuggled soft in my duvet
Pictures of me shooting and scoring
Like any other would do.
Dancing they are happy for me to shoot and score,
Twirling they cheer me on.
I feel wonderful and happy
When I dream of that dream I usually fall out of bed.

Joe Pearson

The Team Goalkeeper

Fast asleep in my bunk bed
I dream of being a Liverpool goalkeeper.
Snuggled soft in my comfy bed
Pictures of me saving a goal
Like showing off to the opponent.
Dancing they high-five each other
Twirling they hug each other.
I feel great for saving a goal
When I dream of being the goalkeeper for Liverpool.

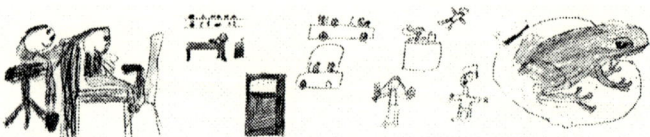

Megan Purvis

The Hairdresser

Fast asleep in my comfy bed
I dream of being a hairdresser.
Snuggled soft in my green and red tent
Pictures of me doing people's hair,
Like cutting hair and putting shape in their hair.
Dancing I chop and cut hair,
Twirling I move from customer to customer.
I feel fantastic
When I dream of being a hairdresser.

Jade Rose

Escaping the Dragon

Fast asleep in my bunk bed with my Teddies
I dream of a dragon after me.
Snuggled soft in my dream cloud
Pictures of me running for my life,
Like a mouse running from a cat.
Dancing I run through trees,
Twirling like a butterfly.
I feel scared
When I dream of a dragon chasing me.

Natalie Smith

Which Job?

On Monday I wanted to be a horse rider.
On Tuesday I wanted to be a baby sitter.
On Wednesday I wanted to be a child minder.
On Thursday I wanted to be a sweet taster.
On Friday I wanted to be a taxi driver.
On Saturday I wanted to be a waitress.
On Sunday I wanted to be a teacher.

Callum St. John

Dream of West Ham

Fast asleep in my snuggly bed
I dream of being a West Ham football player.
Snuggled soft in my covers
Pictures of me scoring exquisite goals
Like the best footballer the world has ever seen.
Dancing they cheer "Go on you Irons!"
Twirling they sing West Ham's theme song.
I feel incredible!!!
When I dream of playing for West Ham.

Joseph St. John

Fantastic Footballer

Fast asleep in my comfortable bed
I dream of being a fantastic footballer.
Snuggled soft, in my excited head
Pictures of footballers scoring incredible goals.
Like cheetahs running at incredible speed
Dancing they celebrate a wonderful goal,
Twirling they cheer for their wonderful team.
I feel like a footballer who plays for wonderful West Ham
When I dream of being a fantastic footballer.

Charlie Ward

Dogs and Cars

Fast asleep cuddled up with my dog
I dream of racing cars.
Snuggled soft in Brandy's bed
Pictures of cars
Like Brandy running after the cars.
Dancing they drive up and down,
Twirling they skid down the track.
I feel good
When I dream of Brand's Hatch.

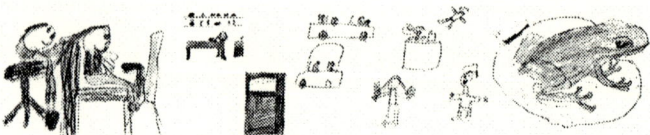

Katie Whybrow

Tightrope Walker

When I grow up I want to be a tightrope walker in a bright, colourful circus because I am really good at balancing in lots of fascinating, fun, fantastic sports. Most of all I would like everybody clapping me on and having a bright red sparkly costume on. Then being up very high and then boing, boing, boing, on to the trampoline.

Alexandra Wright

Cloud Hopping

Fast asleep in my cuddly bed
I dream of flying in the air.
Snuggled soft in my pink and purple bed
Pictures of me bumping into the aeroplanes as I go
Like a bird flying away.
Dancing I jump from cloud to cloud
Twirling I twisted on a cloud.
I feel incredible
When I dream of flying in the air!

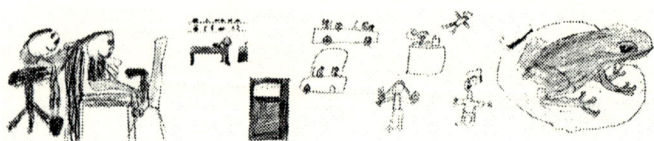

Rory Young

___

Exploring Africa

I was asleep, when I woke up I knew I had a dream and it all
started when I was exploring the jungle in Africa. A native came
up to me and said "Would you like to look after animals in the
safari park?"

"Okay," I said and I followed the native. At last I saw a great big
park with loads of animals and I think my favourite animal is the
monitor lizard, and I said "That's a nice animal," and I enjoyed it
all so much that's what I would like to do in the future. I would
like to explore the world and discover new wildlife that no-one's
found before. I could write a book about them.

CHAPTER 5

Class 4 Dreams

James Austin-Rooth

A New Room

I've been dreaming and dreaming of having a bigger room. And soon my dream will come true. In the summer we are getting an extension built and I'll have Mum's room.

When I get my new room I will decorate it with lots of football things; stickers, posters and wallpaper all about Fulham Football Club. I'm really excited about my new room, it will be great.

Katie Bishop

I want to be...

Monday I wanted to be a baker.
Tuesday I wanted to be a waitress.
Wednesday I wanted to be a cleaner.
Thursday I wanted to be a singer.
Friday I wanted to be a teacher.
Saturday I wanted to be a mechanic
Sunday I am going to be a writer.
And I will!

Laura Boon

My Dream Catcher

My dream catcher works night after night,
Holding any dream that gives me a fright.

My dream catcher hangs on my bedroom wall
It hangs there for days and nights but it will never fall.

It protects me and catches my dreams all night through.
It hangs there all feathery and bright blue.

My dream catcher is my night time friend,
I sleep and dream amazing dreams right to the end.

Callum Bushell

Dreams Acrostic

Dreams are lovely, I love dreams.
Rotten dreams are called nightmares.
Ears are listening for what dreams people say.
After you awake you cannot remember your dreams.
Mums wake us up from lovely dreams
Sun comes up - we wake up!

Hollie Colville

Dreams Acrostic

Dreams can be good, but sometimes bad.
Remembering them in the morning is very hard.
Every dream might mean something, I don't know.
Apples falling off trees,
Magical fairies flying around fairyland.
Scary dreams make me shiver!

Steffan Cook

Daydreams and Night Dreams

I was mowing the lawn and I had a daydream. I thought the lawn
mower was a formula one car. I was racing past everyone. I
changed into gear five and ... "Steffan! Steffan! wake up. You
have done the whole garden". By then it was time for bed. I
finally got to sleep and I had another dream. I got thrown into
the forest and I heard a noise. It was a purring sound. Then I saw
some glowing red eyes. The sound came louder and louder. The
glowing red eyes were a panther. It scratched me and it scratched
me again.   But when I woke up, it was my Dad tapping me on
the hand in time for school.

Dione Dempster

My Future

I dream about what I want to be in the future. Last night I dreamed about being a pop star. Tuesday night I dreamed about being an actor because my Dad said he wants me to have lots of money and look after him when he gets older. On Wednesday night I dreamed about being a person who looks after dogs. I really like dogs, I did have a dog and some ducks. Now I've got a parrot called Billy. On Thursday night I dreamed of being a vet but I'm not too sure - I don't like snakes. On Friday night I dreamed of being a midwife, that's what my Mum is.

Cameron Farmer

The Trap

One night I had a really strange dream. In my dream there was a chair, a bed and a boot. The chair knocked on the door and I knew it was him so I hid under my bed. Then the evil chair smashed the door down. "Where is that pest?" said the chair. They went. I got out from under the bed and followed but they caught me; it was a trap. As they have a trap they will get me even if I'm at home. So I am moving to my Dad's old house.

Harry Grassom

Dreams at Night

Dreams are little stories that your brain tells you at night
Remembering them is often tricky.
Everyone has at least five dreams a night.
Adventures, exploring and hundreds of other things
                                happen in your dream.
Most of the time when you wake up your last dream
                                hasn't finished.
Sometimes people have frightening dreams called nightmares.

Kyle Gurr

Prehistoric Nightmare

One night I had a nightmare, it was about dinosaurs. Me and my brothers were running from a raptor. We found a hole and jumped in. Then we realised that we were in a raptor nest, so we decided to run! We went behind a tree then we went up the tree. The branch that we were sitting on broke and I woke up.

Isabella Harris

The Chocolate Dream

The other day I found a map and I was sure that it was showing you the way to some chocolate bar. Well not just a chocolate bar, a very big one. Soon I found myself following the map; I didn't want to but it just looked so yummy. It didn't look that far away, but it was that far away, unless I had taken the long route.

Then straight in front of me WAS THE CHOCOLATE BAR. I ran to it as fast as I could until … STOP! It was Mum. "Izzy, are you day dreaming?" she said calmly. Then I knew it was just a dream, but it didn't stop me from going to get a chocolate bar out of the fridge.

Laura Hill

A Poem about a Dream

I was swimming in the sea
It was only Dad and me.
Along came a whale
He was reading the Daily Mail.
We were so shocked
We went to the dock
And warmed up with a cup of tea.

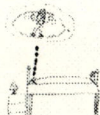

Simeon Jankowski

Dreams Acrostic

Dreams can be really terrifying, really funny, or exciting.
Really funny ones are interesting and obviously funny.
Exciting ones are fun and in the morning I hate it
                  when Mum comes and wakes me up.
And the terrifying ones wake me up in the middle of the
                          night so I can't get to sleep.
My dreams are usually funny or exciting.
So now you know what dreams are like.

Chris Jones

My Nightmare

My dream is a frightful dream, a dream that's really scary. Some dreams can be nice, funny, exciting ones, but not mine.

It was an outdoor birthday party and we were playing 'pin the tail on the donkey'. Then something was controlling my hand and it was this way and that way. The pin on the tail got poked through a hose, the water squirted a beehive. I tried to throw the hose away, but my hands were frozen solid! Suddenly the bees changed direction, my arms and legs unfroze. I ran to the door, but it disappeared and everything around me seemed to disappear.

Then the dream stopped and I could see bees everywhere but this was just an image.

Elaine Kemp

Dreaming Acrostic

Dreams are as dreamy as a creamy ice-cream.
Rare dreams are dreams that make you want to scream.
Extremely horrible you may say,
A nice dream will make you want to stay.
More dreams you may want.
I think you would like a dreamy dream not a screamy dream.
Night: I go to my bed and fall asleep into a dream.
Good dreams are dreamy today.

Jonty Kenward

Flying Poem

Last night I had a lovely dream and I was a bird
Flying through the sky, like birds do of course.
I met lots of other birds that fly in the sky.
The dream ended when my Dad woke me up.

A Nightmare

Last night I had a nightmare about Jesus and God and everyone I know. Jesus and everyone lived in a castle. Jesus had been naughty. He had not taught us anything!

God was really angry. He was to give us a punishment. He did warn us. The next day he was going to give us the punishment. The punishment was to blow up the castle!

Everybody rushed outside. Kayleigh, who wasn't at school that day, saw everybody rushing about. She asked me what was happening. I told her about the punishment. She gasped. Then we got a pair of magic purple fingers. You had to run for 10 seconds with the fingers on, then you would fly. But we were all safe. In the end we all lived in our own parents' houses.

Victoria Leigh

Dreams Acrostic

Dreams are wonderful, you can dream about anything.
Remind yourself dreams are fun to think about.
Even dreaming about the clouds and thinking they
                                            are candyfloss.
Adventures are a good thing to have in your dreams.
Make it up as you go along, that is adventurous.
Some dreams are so exciting you don't want to wake up.

Alan Luckhurst

Locked Out

One dark, misty night I had a bad dream and I am going to tell you my dream. One night Daddy and I were off to a disco. We were in our best clothes and were wearing our smartest dancing shoes. The disco was at a big hall. Daddy and I travelled by car to the disco.

When we arrived at the disco we got out of the car. After that we started to walk to the hall. When we reached the hall where the disco was being held, we found that the doors were locked. A little while later we found that the windows were also locked. When we turned around and started to walk back to the car, we saw a wolf who was about to eat us. My Daddy started to fight the wolf whilst I went to hide from it. At my hiding spot I found twenty pieces of meat and this gave me a brilliant idea. I was going to throw the pieces of meat to the wolf and then run quickly to the car. I started to throw the meat to the wolf and ran to the car with Daddy. Finally we left to go home, exhausted.

Rebecca Mansell

Monsters

I wonder what I shall dream tonight -
Will it be of fairies or monsters to fight?
As I drift off to sleep I am in the dentist's chair,
The dentist saying "I am going to pull out all your teeth
And cut off your hair".
I scream and shout,
But no sound comes out.
Suddenly I awake, confused and tired.
I think it was a dream, but that dentist should be fired!

Daire McGivern

Dream Game

One night I had a very nice dream. I dreamed about me going to see Liverpool Football Club. The first person I met was Steve Finnan. He took me onto the pitch and I met the team. They took me to the pub with them and I had a bag of crisps. Later on Fulham Football Club arrived and the game began. It was a great start, Liverpool scored first so the score was 1-0. After a while Fulham managed to get a goal so that score was 1-1. Soon the final whistle blew and they went on to penalties but no-one won before I woke up.

Danielle North

The Clown

One night I dreamt about a clown, he kept on telling jokes. I didn't even laugh but people kept on laughing but then the clown called me up on his stage, and asked if I could sing a song about a clown pulling faces with tongues poking out. I tried to think about a song but then all the people started laughing. I got so embarrassed I went bright red. I started to sing but the clown said I was rubbish at singing a song so I ran off the stage.

Next I went to a stall where there was china. I broke an old lady figure but then suddenly I woke up and found out it wasn't true. I've always thought dreams were true but I've learnt that they aren't true. I tried to ask my Mum and Dad if dreams were true or not but I found it out for myself for once.

Danni Packman

When I am Dreaming

Sometimes I daydream,
Sometimes I wish,
Sometimes I dream that I have cream round my lips.
Daydreaming is lovely, you feel
All drowsy, all sleepy, all tired and relaxed.
It's time to dream, it's time to relax.
What is the time?
It's quarter past nine.
I am going to sit in the corner
To dream about chocolate chip ice-cream.
See you tomorrow.
Bye, bye.

Matthew Russell

The Light

On one mysterious night I had a weird dream. I saw a light glowing in the dark. It was a glowing stone, shining like armour, shining in the sky. I thought I was dreaming. Then it fell on a rock. The light shone once more. Then it went out and I felt sad for two weeks. The light had made me happy and I couldn't see it now. Then one night I looked out of the window. It was back! I felt happy once more.

Bethany Simpson

I Want to be a Butterfly

I close my eyes and drift
Into a peaceful place.
I dream of being a butterfly
That can fly up into space.
Not too high, not low
I'll flutter to and fro.
Smelling flowers as I go.
Pink, red, purple, yellow, green and blue.
My dream is coming to an end,
The next day will begin again.

Charlotte Thatcher

Lunch with Mary-Kate and Ashley

I felt nice and warm with the sun beaming on my face. I could hear the waves against the shore. All of a sudden I recognised some voices. I put my sunglasses on and my hand over my forehead to take the glare out of my eyes. There before me stood my favourite actresses, Mary Kate and Ashley Olsen. I felt so excited and so happy I could not believe my eyes. Ashley asked "Excuse me, is there a nice restaurant nearby?"
I replied "Oh yes, there is a lovely quaint restaurant, let me take you there." On the way we were having a lovely chat.

Before long we arrived at the Fountain Restaurant. They invited me to have lunch with them. We sat at the table with a lovely view, the restaurant also had a good atmosphere. I had a cold lemonade and Mary Kate and Ashley had the same. It was very refreshing. We ate some pasta and talked and laughed some more. It was the best day of my life and I was so glad that I had met them both. We said goodbye and left the restaurant.

While I was walking back to the beach, my vision went blurry. I found myself lying down in my back garden with the sun beaming on my face and the sound of the waterfall from the pond. I heard my Mum calling to me to come in for lunch. I realised what a lovely dream I had had.

William Thirkell

Playing for England at Nineteen

In ten years' time I hope to play for the England Cricket team and win all my matches. Most of all I hope to captain England and win the World Cup in 2019 which will be my first World Cup. I hope to get the world record of wickets in test and one-day international. I also hope to get the highest test score of over 400, which was made by Brian Lara.

I want to go all around the world to places like Australia, South Africa, Zimbabwe, Kenya, Namibia, Holland, Canada, West Indies, India, Pakistan, Bangladesh, New Zealand and Sri Lanka. That's what I want to do when I'm nineteen.

Katie Thorn

Clouds

Last night the lightning struck.
It really was just my bad luck.
In bed I listened to the rain,
Tapping on the window pane.

I started daydreaming about the clouds.
Sometimes they look really proud,
But right now the clouds are angry,
And are starting to growl … at me!

When the clouds are in a very good mood,
They are nowhere to be seen.
That's the time that we like the most,
When we hop in the car and go to the coast.

It's getting quite dark now,
And I can only hear a distant growl.
That's the last of the lightning.
That really was quite frightening.

Winning the Cup

When I was asleep I dreamt that I played for Charlton and I scored and we won the FIFA Cup. We beat Fulham. I held up the trophy and the crowd shouted. In the morning I woke up.

Ben White

In my Room

One day I dreamed of an alien coming in my room. Then I watched it turn blue. It turned into a ghost and googly eyes came up to me and stared in my face. Then I screamed! I was really scared! Then the ghost suddenly turned all blue and screamed. Thousands of hoops came up in the air, I stood under the hoops. I turned into a zombie. My friend stood under the hoops with me. We all changed into zombies. Then I woke up and never had that dream again.

Callum Willson

Red Suzuki

I dream of buying myself a motorbike when I am older. I hope
to have a powerful red, shiny Suzuki. I will have red leathers and
a helmet to match my bike. I will go everywhere on it during the
summer, but I also want a car that I can use in the winter when
the weather is wet and miserable.

CHAPTER 6

Dreams of Class 5

Sophie Arthurs

Holiday Dreams

I was on holiday in France having a lovely time, and my sister Amy and I were sleeping together on this pull-out bed. I was getting to sleep and my sister Amy, who is disabled, was still awake. Amy was playing with her rattle, while I was dreaming a lovely dream. Suddenly, my dream changed into a horrible dream.

I was in a court room, and I felt like I was in a Wonderland court room. It had flowers all around the place, and on the seats there were cushions which had fur on them. The next second it felt like somebody was standing on my head, but really it was my sister sitting on me. I was pushing and shoving and trying to get her off, but it was no use - she wouldn't come off. Then I heard a sound that sounded like a toilet flush. I heard my Mum's voice, she said, "Amy, it's time you went to sleep," and she picked Amy off me. As soon as she got off me I turned over and stretched. All of a sudden I woke up. That was the worst dream I had when I was on holiday.

Ross Ayling

The Visitor

I woke up to a nice sunny Sunday morning, I jumped out of bed, pulled open the curtains and went downstairs to have breakfast. On Sundays I go and play for my local football club, Bearsted Under 10s. Today the coach had said there was a special visitor coming to watch us. I couldn't wait to see who he was. When I got there I saw a long white limo. He must be special! Then the limo door opened, first out came some bodyguards, then out came... the Head Coach of Chelsea Football Club. I was shocked and amazed. My eyes caught sight of him with my mouth wide open. Apparently he came to see our game against Vinters Park, and pick a boy to join Chelsea Under 10s. So I really needed to play at my best. It has been my dream to play for Chelsea.

Night Dream

This is a dream that I have every night:
On my way to buy a horse I saw a chestnut horse tied up by a
chain. It looked so sad as it was on its own. I went inside and said
to the man, "Is that chestnut horse outside for sale?"
The man asked, "What horse?"
I said, "The one tied to a chain." He said, "Can you show me this
horse?"
I replied, "Yes of course."
He said, "This isn't one of my horses. My horses are all inside."
I thought it couldn't be anybody else's because all along the road
there were shops. Luckily he let me have it for free. I was so
happy. Then all of a sudden, the chestnut horse, which I had
called Roxsy, reared up as a car zoomed up behind us. I told
Roxsy to calm down and she did. The driver slowed down and I
had a quick glimpse of the number plate.

When I got home I put Roxsy in her stable and went out to buy a
saddle and bridle. I quickly drove home, took the saddle and
bridle, tied Roxsy up and then put them on her. She was really
good. I jumped up on her and walked her round the ring. We did
a bit of a canter - I did slow her down as I walked her round the
road. Then she got scared again by a car so I had a good look at
the number plate. Then I fell off her as she didn't calm down.
When I woke up I remembered all of it, but most of all I
remembered Roxsy.

Jack Bennett

Animal Business

One day I walked out into the field to see my animals. They were all out grazing in the field. Some of them were still inside eating. I had exactly ninety-five goats, and me and my friend Will were just cleaning them out. It was hard! We had lots of helpers and volunteers.

First I went out at half past eight to feed them their breakfast, then they needed to be groomed. Also to have their feet checked for footrot which can make them limp. After that they could be let out. Later on when I came back to check them, seventeen had gone!

I was walking around in the field looking for them when my mobile rang. It was a lady - her garden was being trampled by my goats, and they were eating her flowers!! In the evening I went back. Earlier I had brought the goats back safely. I just have to put six more away now. Then I have to mix the food and they are done.

Later on I went to bed. The next day I woke up. I thought, I don't have goats, it was just a goat sanctuary next to my house.

Dharamvir Bhambra

The Battle

My family and I were going to the beach, but we did not know that the beach was not there any more. So when we got there it was a battlefield, and some people were waiting for us. They wanted to kill us, so we took the challenge and we were fighting.

My sister slipped on the floor and I went to see if she was okay, but they were going to kill me, I knew that they were. So I stuck out my sword and killed them. I got my sister up and we started fighting. My family and I killed everyone, and then I said, "I will kill the leader of them." I was fighting the leader, who was called Sam. I was fighting him and I could not cut him. At last I killed him but something weird happened. Someone came and we killed them and won.

Amy Carter-Rees

Marshmallow Dream!

A long time ago, when I was nine to be precise, I had a good day
at school but a terrible thing was about to happen that night. I
went to bed at nine pm and a dream was about to happen.
Suddenly everything started to spin. Every single thing fell off my
shelves. At last it stopped and I felt relaxed.
Mum started screaming, "Aahh."
"What's wrong, Mum?" I said, furiously.
"Your Dad has just vanished," she replied.
"You must be kidding me," I said again. Mum and I ran outside
and stopped. Everything had turned into marshmallow except
people and animals, just everything else.

We had forgotten about Dad's disappearance. We were too
amazed at the marshmallow. Mum took the first step and had a
bit of the tree leaf. "Mmmmm," Mum said. So I had my first step
and Mum gave me her remaining marshmallow leaf. Then
suddenly Mum and I heard, "Aarrgh."
Mum said, "That was Dad. Quick, follow Dad's screams."
Suddenly we came up to a maze. "I am no good at mazes," I said.
"Nor am I," Mum said. Then she said, "Eat the maze, quick."
Eventually we came to Dad, then I woke up. I went up to Dad
and gave him a cuddle.

Holly Davidson

Me and My Lion

One day in hot, sunny Africa, me and my Mum were walking down the dusty road to the market. As we were looking at the stalls, Mum spotted the bakery stall, but out of the corner of my eye I saw a man selling newborn lion cubs.

"Mum, Mum," I cried, tugging at my Mum's arm. "Look - can I have a lion cub please?" I asked in my sweetest voice.

"As it is your birthday in two days it can be an early birthday present from me, your Dad and Max," said my Mum.

"Thank you," I said, getting all excited.

I asked the man if he had any boy lion cubs. The man lifted up two female cubs, and removed some hay, and under the hay was the last and youngest male cub. The man who ran the stall gently picked up the cub and handed it to me. He drifted off to sleep in my arms.

"Look, Mum, he likes me. I want to call him Russell," I whispered. When we got home, Dad and Max were quite surprised, but happy when they saw Russell.

"Dad, where can we keep Russell?" I asked.

"Not in the house!" said Max.

"How about we keep him in the garden shed?" Suggested my Dad. "Okay," I agreed.

So the next day me, my Mum and my Dad spend most of the day making Russell's house, and from then on Russell and I spent all day, every day, together. In my dreams...

138

Bronwyn Davis

I'm Going to a Place Like Alice in Wonderland

First I walked into a place with doughnuts. Then I saw a girl
walking past. I said, "Hello." She said "Hello," back. I asked if
she knew where I was, but she said, "No, sorry."
"Do you know where to find a place where there is a
trampoline?" I said.
"No, but shall we go together? Okay," she said. Then we found a
waterfall on the way there. We sat down and had a cup of water
and some doughnuts. After all of that, we kept going.

"It is a long way," I said.
"It is!" Hannah (the girl in my dream) said. Then we closed our
eyes and suddenly we opened them and we were there - at the
trampoline. On the trampoline there were some of my friends,
Kim, Gem, Ellis and Amy. After we had a play, suddenly Hannah
disappeared, it was so weird!
Then we went off to find a couple of beds to sleep in, but we
couldn't, so we laid down on some doughnuts. They smelt nice -
and tasted nice as well. They had sugar on them. Then suddenly
my friends disappeared. I heard them call, "Bronwyn," but it was
my Mum. I was in bed - but I had a dougnut in my hand. Was it
true or not?

Lloyd Dempster

The Incredible Family

I've just woken up and I'm going downstairs. Mum's there with a friend, chatting. I'm just about to step down the stairs, but I see my dog, Bella - she's hurt. I'm trying to get downstairs, but I trip and grow wings and fly down the stairs safely, and Bella grew wings too, but then our wings went.

My family and I are going on a bungee jump, but we forgot to do our seatbelts and we fall off. As we are in the air, I get out my wand and put wings on Mum, Dad and Dione. But now I have no power to give myself any wings, so I was going to fall on the trampoline in my garden, but it disappeared. So I fall in a river and Mum and Dad save me with their wings.

We go back home and our wings go. Then we go to Burger King, but it had been abandoned. All the food is on the tables, so we eat all the food. Then we hear a noise. We see a big, dark shadow. Then a DINOSAUR comes rushing out. He ROARS and then we run as fast as our legs will carry us with our hearts beating faster than our legs. Then my Dad trips. We go back to save him and see a man that had been killed - he had a gun. My Dad picked it up, then he shoots the dinosaur and he falls on the ground making it shake. Dust is everywhere, and everyone claps for us and we get known as The Incredibles. Then I wake up.

Charlie Easton

The Haunted Mansion

One day on Hallowe'en I was getting dressed into my Hallowe'en
costume, and then I saw something quite strange. I saw another
door, because I only had one door. I went through it. I found
myself in a graveyard and at the end of the graveyard there was a
giant gate. I went through it. It came out into a haunted mansion.
I didn't know what to do, so I looked all round apart from the
last door. I went in and to my astonishment I saw a ghost trying
to kill my Mum.
"Go and save the treasure," said my Mum to save me.
"Okay," I said. So I went down into the cellar and there it was in
a big black box. I got it but the ghost was chasing after me. I ran
and ran as fast as I could. I could see the door, I opened it and
put the big black box of treasure down. As quick as thunder my
Mum turned back so she wasn't dead. Then I woke up and found
myself in bed. I went downstairs and saw my Mum. Straight away
I gave her a bigggg cuddle. We lived happily ever after.

Liam Elliot

The Monster Hunters

It was a normal day like any other day except I was on an island with my crew, the monster hunters. We were up early for breakfast, and then we got our gear and went looking for monsters. We had no luck until we saw three big shadows on the other side of our tent. We went slowly with the net around the corner, looked at the monsters, and found they were hamsters. Then we heard some weird sounds. We knew where they were coming from.

Three hunters came out of the ground. We asked them what they were looking for. They said hamsters. Luckily, we had three. We gave them the hamsters, but they escaped. The hamsters and the hunters ran around the tent and then they went inside. We saw the three big shadows again. I said, "What is happening?" But the shadows heard me and one of them peeped round the corner. We ran for our lives, but they chased us and they were catching up. They jumped at my crew. My crew were down. I was still running with the monsters behind, and then I woke up.

Esther Faulkner

Ballet Dream

I am standing in the wings of the stage and I am very nervous.
My turn to dance is getting closer every minute. My teachers and
dancing friends keep encouraging me. My turn finally comes and
I run on to the stage...

I dance and dance, spinning and pointing my toes. I suddenly
realise that I'm enjoying myself! Spin and point, I'm giggling to
myself now. There is nothing to be scared about after all. I spin
and run off. I'm not on for a while, so I can have a drink and
maybe something to eat. At last the final person is on. I run to
get changed into my finale costume. It's wonderful. I then hurry
to the side to prepare for the finale. Everyone starts walking on
to the stage, but my teacher calls me back and asks me to do a
special dance after the bow. Of course I say yes, and run after the
others onto the stage. After the bow I do my own solo dance.
Then another bow. The audience go wild, throwing flowers and
money onto the stage. I bowed again and run off. I am really
pleased with myself as my parents will be. I suddenly hear a voice
calling "Esther, Esther, Esther." Then I woke up and found it
had all been a dream.

Paul Figg

More Bad News

Once, when I was five or six, I dreamt that I was going to the park to have a picnic. When we got there with my Mum, Dad and my sister this girl came up to me and said, "My name is Rose. Can I live with you?"
I said, "Ask my Mum or Dad." Before she did ask them a monster ran into the park and hit the swings which collapsed. My Dad lit a fire, so the monster ran away. My Mum and Dad said yes to Rose. When we got back Rose tried pushing me out of the window. Before I could open my eyes a superhero was standing there with his hands on his hips. The superhero, called Flash, picked up a sword and chopped off Rose's head. No blood came out. No liver was there, but then it struck me. There was no liver or blood there because she was a ROBOT. Then there was even more bad news. The monster came back for more, but it was no problem for Flash, he just flicked him, and he died. That's the end of my dream.

Ben Flint

The Demon Attackers

It was a sunny day in L.A. I was on a helicopter (because I was a secret agent) and two demons jumped on. One hit one of my guards and the other demon ripped his guts out. Another demon was on a crane and went right next to the helicopter, and grabbed the dead guard's gun as yet another demon strangled another guard. I grabbed the dead guard's gun and shot the demon that was on the crane and it smashed into smithereens. The other two demons pushed me off the helicopter and then my guards started to chase me as well.

I ran along a path between two lakes and then saw a large shape moving in the water. The water was too murky to make out what the thing was. Just then the thing leapt out of the water. It was the king of the demons, 100-foot tall, heavily muscled and big boned. It had scars all over its face. It tried to crush me but missed. My guard that survived shot the demon. (I thought it was a bit of a waste, because it would have been as effective as trying to knock down Nelson's Column with a fly swat.) The demon got angry and squashed the guard. I ran past to gates which were metal, and chopped the two demons that were chasing me into tiny pieces, and tripped the big king demon. He cracked his head open and that was the end of him. Then another demon (the one who squashed the guard) pounced. I got my gun out. And I woke up. It wasn't a sunny day in L.A. and I wasn't a secret agent. I was Ben Flint in bed under a quilt in Kent on a rainy, cold winter night.

Robynne Ghent

Chocolate Dream

As I walked through a forest I came to a waterfall made of hot
chocolate. Along the way I saw a trampoline. I got on it. I
jumped and it turned into chocolate, and I gobbled it up. Then I
came across a swimming pool. I dived in - the swimming pool
was made of hot chocolate. Then I went into a house made of
chocolate. The TV was boring so I ate it. Dinner was lamb with
chocolate potatoes with chocolate sauce. I wished I was back
home after dinner, I was very sick.

I went outside - some people took me to Chocolate City, it took
ages. The stepping stones were made out of wine gums.
Everything else was made out of chocolate. We walked through
the city. It was nice but a bell rang, I had to go when the bell
struck. So I ran out of the city. The chocolate was all I had left so
I ate it all, but it just came back. I gave up on eating the
chocolate. I cried and cried. Then this chocolate caterpillar said,
"Why are you crying, little girl?"
"I'm not little, I'm big."
"You have shrunk, little girl."
"Oh no, how will I get back to being big?"
"Well, eat the chocolate button." So I did. The taste was lovely, it
melted so slowly in your mouth. It was lovely and it made me big.
It was great. Then I woke up. It was all a dream - but in my hand
was a chocolate button so I wonder. I'm curious to know
whether it was a dream or not.

146

Kieran Hoadly

My Dream

One night I had a dream, and this is how it went. I was about forty-five years old and I had an assistant about twenty-eight years old. I was inventing a new machine. This machine was very different from any other because it can go underwater, on water, on land and in the air. I had all the parts I needed in my lab and I knew how I was going to build it, so I started.

First, I had to build the frame of it which was going to be hard. "Okay, let's start," I said. We started with the front and worked our way back. My assistant held the parts while I carefully welded them together. It took a long time to put it together. Next, we started on the outside which would take even longer as each part had an exact place. The outside was hard, especially the roof. Then we started on the engine which was very complicated and was going to be tiring. Once we had finished we did inside which was a bit easier. The machine was ready. We decided to test it. We tested it in the air first. We decided I should fly it. I was in the air, "Oh, it's going smoothly," I said through the headset. Then I heard the alarm.

"What..? Something's wrong... I'm losing height!" I shouted. I was about to crash. "Aahhhhh!" I yelled. But then as I was about to hit the ground... I woke up.

A Ballerina

At home I was thinking about something and I fell asleep and
had a dream. The dream was in the future, it was what I would
like to be when I am older. I dreamt about me being a dancer,
but a particular dancer - a ballet dancer. I would dance in
theatres all around the world. As I go to dance I also have a
holiday. When I went to Australia I had to stop at America to get
a digital camera. So I got back onto the plane and went to
Australia. When I got there I had over two hours to get ready for
the big show. I wore a glittery dress and I was on blocks like a
ballerina. I did the big show and at the end they all clapped. I felt
so happy and then, I suddenly fell over, then my Mummy
shouted up to me and suddenly, I was in my room.

Matilda Knowler

An Amazing Dream

I was looking in my wardrobe for my tracksuit when I was sucked into a swirl of colour. Suddenly I fell and landed onto a field of candyfloss. There were little people made of liquorice everywhere, dancing and playing together. Little dolly mixtures were on bushes instead of flowers. I ventured further and saw a farm with chickens laying creme eggs, and sheep with candyfloss wool. This world was amazing - a world of sweets. I continued to stare until I saw a purple door with golden stars and yellow flowers. I was curious and opened it. I cautiously entered into the next world.

It was amazing! It was hard to think what this was at first, but suddenly it came to me. It was the inside of an Egyptian pyramid! I slowly strolled around staring at the ancient hieroglyphics. All the pictures looked so carefully done and accurate that I longed to be able to do this. Eventually I found another door, next to the chamber of the pharaoh (but I didn't know which one). This one was strange because it wasn't door-shaped, it was diamond-shaped. I was in a hot air balloon going over a lake which was twinkling away with lilies, ducks, swans and geese. I just wanted to stay there and wait forever, but I knew I had to go into the next portal and back to my room. I slowly went into an oval door to another place. I was suddenly in the colourful vortex once again, twirling and spinning down the tunnel coming to an eventual stop. I slowly opened my eyes and I was being shaken by my Mum. It was really all a dream.

Patrick Knowles

Mutated

I was walking along at night with Paul. We were walking back to
my house when we saw this old man. The first thing I noticed
were his eyes, they were going red. Paul and I went up to him but
the next thing I knew was that he'd just mutated into a goblin
and was attacking Paul. Luckily Paul had also mutated and had
wings. By now, I was totally confused. Next it was my turn... I
was transforming. When I'd transformed, I was a super-fast
Ninja and was perfect at ju-jitsu. That's when everyone joined in.
What a sight, I thought. There were mutants with wings, clubs,
boomerangs and super sharp teeth. The funny thing is that some
people still had blue eyes and blond hair so I could just tell one
from the other. Getting on with the dream, we'd just killed the
last of the evil mutant thingies when Professor X from the X-
men came up to us and said it was mutant disease, that if your
heart was not pure good, you turned evil. That's when I woke up
to find myself in a mutant suit which I'd never seen before.

James Leigh

Fire!

There was a small spark on the landing one night. Suddenly it set
alight the landing. I got up to have a drink. I opened the door of
my room and saw the fire. Suddenly a flash of fire flew into my
room, but it went out. I slammed the door and ripped the sheets
off my bed and shoved them at the bottom of the door. Then,
with difficulty, I ripped the mattress up and threw it out of the
window. Then I jumped out of it too. I kept on falling - falling -
falling - falling... Suddenly I landed in a ring of fire, and in front
of me was a porthole. I entered. This time I started spinning
round - round - round and round then I... woke up.

Jamie Leith

A Dream Heading to Mars

I had a dream of heading to the planet Mars. It was the
countdown: 10, 9, 8, 7, 6, 5, 4, 3, 2, 1, blast off. A big explosion,
shaking the Earth. As I went up in the air, past the sky and
disappearing from view, I shot up past the moon and saw Mars,
but the legs on this ship could not come out. The only way the
ship could land was by crashing into the planet. I pulled the lever
up and closed my eyes, but then smash. I had just survived the
crash. As I got out of my ship, I began to jump. I felt that I was
flying, but I had a big problem. It was how to fix my ship because
the engine had been broken when I went into Mars.

As I was walking I saw little aliens coming towards me. They
thought that I was a robot because of my spacesuit. I came closer
to them. One of the aliens pulled my arm and brought me to a
city. I wanted to have a look, but all the aliens went to get
something. They came back with some tools and they ran to my
ship and tried to fix it. One of them said, "Where do you come
from?" I said, "Earth."
All of a sudden, they were very mad. "We want to rule Earth,"
one of the aliens said. "Why?" I asked.
"Because people on Earth steal our Mars bars," all the aliens said.
I ran so fast back to my ship and set off. The aliens did a good
job of fixing my ship, but all of a sudden one of the aliens got on
board and said, "Do you want your Mars bars?" I just woke up
and saw my Mum offering me a Mars bar.
"I must have fallen asleep." I said.

James McDonald

The Dream of Hot-air Balloons

I dreamt that I would own a hot air balloon. This is how it started:

I went to this place where there were loads of little party balloons, then suddenly they all turned into hot air balloons. I fell over because people pushed me aside. I got up and the strangest thing happened. The hot air balloons doubled and then tripled in size. Everyone went quiet in amazement. One by one the balloons took off with advertising on them. When the balloons took off they all fell out of the sky. Everybody rushed over to where they fell. The people who owned the balloons said, "Keep away, they're haunted." They packed up the balloons but they came out of their bags. Everybody ran away and went home.

Once again the balloons took off and followed them. Everybody hid, and then the balloons decided to find them. They chased the people. The balloons had guns. They had faces and they looked mean. The balloons managed to kill some of the people and then they chucked out a bomb and killed everybody. I got so frightened I woke up.

Daniel Morgan

Escaping the Wolves

It was dawn and my friend and I were going through a footpath
in the woods. It was dark and dingy and the trees were waving.
We suddenly got lost and it was starting to get darker. While we
were walking through the woods, we heard the wolves howling.
My friend and I were nervous. We heard something shuffling in
the bush. Then out came the fiercest-looking man with long teeth
and grey skin. A pack of wolves came running out and were
chasing us. We couldn't run any faster and they were catching us
up. Then we fell into a six-feet deep hole. We felt breathing on
our heads - it was a bat. We had run into a dark and gloomy cave.
We started running. All I could hear was my heart thumping.
Then suddenly I heard a roooaaarrr. It was a man eating a lion. I
was in shock and we ran for our lives. I lost my friend and I
heard q-q-q-q-q-q-q-q-q. I woke up and it was my alarm clock.

Ben Pearson

The Long and Winding Road

I am slowly walking along on a far, winding road. The only
sounds I hear are the rustling of leaves, the howling of the wind,
the swaying of the trees and my heart thumping, thumping,
thumping. I slowly walked as fear sent shivers down my spine.

Then the ground starts opening, the ground starts shaking, fire
was roaring beneath me about to turn me to a crisp, but I keep
walking on thin air. Hills start mounting on the ground as high as
mountains, higher than clouds. As wide as fields with millions of
people in, and I fall up and down, up and down. I start nearing
the end of the long and winding road, but a wolf with a frizzy
dark coat, as black as the sky, starts chasing me. The wolf was
ripping at my heels, I drew closer to death's dark door. I felt the
hair on the back of my head stand on end. I was sweating all
over, but I end my journey and... I wake up.

Changing Scenes

"Ouch!" I said. I had suddenly appeared in a long, dark cave with a flaming wooden stick in my right hand. I was creeping along the cave, my heart was pounding faster each five seconds. I gradually started to run until...

"That's strange," I said feebly. I had no idea how, but the cave had turned into a railway track which was filled with bustling people. I walked up to an old woman, "Um... excuse me, can you tell me where I am?" I asked as politely as I could. She didn't answer. She must have heard her train coming because she walked straight past me like I wasn't there! Repeatedly a voice in my head said carry on, it won't hurt. I walked on.

Once again the railway track turned into a beach! It was a blazing hot day. The track was no longer there, instead all I could see was the rest of the beach and the car park! Suddenly I felt my feet sinking. I peered down and saw the tide coming in. I clenched my leg and yanked it out, "Aahhh!" I screamed. I ducked just in time and a football just missed me. "Hey, what was that for?" I said when I had overcome the fact that my head could have had a huge bruise on it. I went to collect the ball when again I found I was walking through an aquatic tunnel with sharks and fish swimming all around me. All I saw was the door at the end. I ran and ran until suddenly I fell. Down and down and down. Thud!! I had crash-landed on my bed. "Atchoo." I opened my eyes and realized it was all a rather silly dream.

Gemma Rogers

My Nightmare

I'm somewhere I have never been before, it feels like the middle of nowhere. There are no trees, no plants, no buildings and no people. Everything looks exactly the same and the grass seems to stretch on for miles and miles. As I run, my trainers thud on the ground. I think to myself, "Haven't I already been here?" but there is no way of telling. Suddenly, I see a dark building. I run up to it and see a huge stone staircase at the front of it. As I climb up, it seems to grow bigger and I grow smaller. It takes forever to reach the top, but when I do I see a huge, old door. I feel nervous as I walk towards it, I reach up and knock three times. Slowly the door creaks open and reveals a long, black-cloaked person with glowing red eyes. For a second I think the cloak is floating in mid-air!

A voice inside the cloak says, "Come in, we're expecting you." "Who's we?" I ask, questioningly. He doesn't answer but I soon find out. Inside the building are more people in black cloaks, they move aside revealing a gaping hole in the middle of the room. Suddenly they start chanting and move slowly towards me. I try to run but I just can't move. It is as if I have a ten-tonne weight on each foot glucing me to the spot. They move slowly towards me, their bony hands outstretched, they clasp on to my shoulder and spin me round to face the hole. I am standing right at the edge of the hole. I feel someone push hard on my shoulder. I feel myself falling, falling, falling into nothingness. Suddenly my eyes snap open, I blink once, twice. I am sitting up in my bed, awake.

Harry Rogers

My Dream of Winning the FA Cup

I have dreamt that in the future I will become a professional
football player. I will play for West Ham and England, and I will
be Captain of West Ham. I will play on the right side of midfield.

West Ham were in the FA Cup Final. We won all our matches
and now we are in the Final. We are against Chelsea. The match
started and I was running up the side with the ball. I passed it to
a team mate and one of the Chelsea players slide-tackled him in
the box. It was a penalty. I stepped up to take the penalty and I
scored. Chelsea had some shots on goal but they did not score.
We won the FA Cup Final. I went up to get the FA cup. The
crowd chanted, "Rogers, Rogers, Rogers." Me and my team
celebrated. We went down the tunnel and the crowd cheered. I
went into the dressing room and Sven Goran Erickson was there.
He asked me if I would be Captain for England against Brazil. I
said, "Yes, okay." I was jumping up and down, I was really
excited, I could not wait. And then I woke up and fell out of bed.

Kimberley Snoad

A Sinking Feeling

"Mum," I shouted, "Vicky and I are going for a walk."
"Okay," she shouted back, and we were off. We were walking through the countryside, all the birds were twittering, the bees were buzzing and there was a gentle breeze passing through our hair. The rabbits were bouncing around, the flowers were blooming. It was perfect until it turned nasty. The clouds broke, a thunderstorm started. Vicky had run away and left me there in the middle of a field.

It was dark, cold, raining and, to make matters worse, I didn't have a coat! I staggered down a rocky path with bits of dagger and metal in it. I fell down a couple of steps and... I landed in a small river. Everybody was watching me, laughing at me and taunting me, I felt helpless. I couldn't scream for help in my dream, it was like I was totally oblivious to the world! All I could hear was, "Ha, ha, look at her. She can't swim, she's stupid, too stupid to even function." Then some of my friends were at the riverbank pointing and laughing at me. Just then, one of my friends said, "Oh well, I've never really liked her anyway."
All the teachers came and said, "Tsk, tsk, she never did her homework."
"No, I agree. She never turned up for swimming lessons either."
Just then, I felt myself sinking and I could hear my heart pumping in my ears and...

William Thew

Skeletons at the Tower

It was a cold, wintry night and I couldn't sleep. The wind was making the trees bang against the windows. Suddenly I was in France on a blazing hot day. A limo came up to the Eiffel Tower, next to where I was sitting. Two bodyguards got out. They each stood either side of the back door. Another bodyguard climbed out, followed by the Queen of England (Queen Victoria). They all started to climb the Eiffel Tower, I followed them up to the top. Suddenly the Queen screamed, her crown had slipped off her head and got stuck on a rail in the middle of the Tower.

I had to think before I acted, but I would have done anything for the Queen. So I walked over to her and said, "I will get your crown, your Majesty." She told me to hurry. I started to climb down, I had a look down and it wasn't far now. Suddenly, skeletons started coming out of the ground and started climbing up! One of them was just about to grab the crown when I slid down, kicked him and took the crown out of his grasp. Whilst I was tying the crown to my belt, I watched one of them smash on the ground, but other skeletons were catching me up. One of them grabbed my leg, then all the others grabbed onto him. I tried to pull myself up, but couldn't. I saw a metal bar loose, so I grabbed it and whacked a skeleton on the head. I kicked his neck and the arms disconnected, all of them fell off although the hands were still grasping my shins tightly. Once I had reached the Queen I gave her the crown and took the hands off my legs. She was just about to say something but then... I woke up.

Luke Whitfield

Open Water

It was Monday 25th April, it was my birthday and I was on a
boat. I was going to swim in the South China Sea. I wanted to
find the world's biggest starfish. I knew where and what it looked
like, it was purple, blue and yellow stripes with a silver gem in the
middle. If you touch it with bare hands it sends a noise only
sharks can hear. We can't hear it because it is a special sound. It's
a bit like a dog whistle. I was swimming along and then I saw it!
A genuine super starfish. I took off my glove and touched the
starfish. Suddenly I feel as if I have burned myself, but it can't
have been the starfish because only...

I think for a bit and say to myself, if only sharks can hear it, how
can I? I look at my body and see I am a shark! In the distance I
could see about twenty figures swimming towards me. I felt really
tense. I would be dripping with sweat if I was out of the water
but I am in the water so I'm already dripping. Suddenly the
twenty figures were swimming towards me full pelt. A shark
came so near I would have been able to touch it. I started to
swim away and succeeded until I looked back - the other
nineteen sharks were swimming towards me like a torpedo.
Suddenly I was petrified because there was a sunken ship inches
in front of me. I tried to slow down but I couldn't and suddenly
thwack. I woke up because I had fallen out of bed. I wondered if
the sharks were real or just a nightmare. I looked out of my
window and saw twenty sharks swimming in a circle...

Dognapped!

It all started when I took my dog, Conway, for a walk. I was happily walking through some woods and I let Conway off his lead. I was throwing his ball and he was fetching it. Then, all of a sudden, he vanished. When I realized, I ran through the woods as fast as I could. Then I found myself at a main road. I saw Conway dodging the cars. When he was at the other side two men jumped out and caught him. "No, he's my dog!" I shouted. As they looked over, a bus pulled in front of me, I felt it was the end of the world, thank goodness it wasn't because then I wouldn't be able to get Conway back.

I ran after the two men. It was no use, I wasn't going to catch up with their super-dooper fast car, was I? Out of the corner of my eye I saw a bike shop. I ran in and said to the owner, "Please can I borrow a bike because my dog has run away and I can't catch up with him without a bike."

"Okay, but..." Before he had finished, I had gone. When I had come out of the bike shop everything changed and I was at the edge of a cliff. The two men suddenly appeared in the car with Conway in the back. One of the men got out of the car and got out a sword and threatened to kill me if I didn't give them five hundred pounds for Conway. As they came nearer I was walking nearer to the edge of the cliff. Suddenly I was falling, falling, falling... then I woke up. When I woke up I heard Conway barking in his sleep. I was so relieved that it wasn't true.

Andrew Woodhams

The Fight

Once upon a time, there was a man. He chased me down the road, he was holding a bat and he was trying to hit me with it, but every time he missed! He keeps chasing me. We run on and on for miles.

I find a gun, laying in the road. I shoot the man, hoping he'll stop. He drops to the floor, but comes back to life after five minutes. I shoot him again, in the leg so he can't chase me any more. I ran on further, turning to look back, I see him get up and come running towards me!

I look down, there's a bat. I pick it up. This man lunges for me, we start fighting. Hitting out at each other. I win! We have five more matches. I win four of the matches, he only wins one. He raises the bat again, so we decide to have another five matches. I win the sixth and seventh match! I also win the eighth match, in fact I win all of them, apart from the last. Whoever wins this, is the ultimate winner. He hits me, I fall, I get up and throw the bat. It connects. He goes down like a sack of potatoes.

I keep on looking at him, waiting for him to get up. He doesn't. I am the winner! Yeah! Yeah! Yeah! The alarm clock blares in my ear, time to get up.

CHAPTER 7

Class 6 Dreams

Stephanie Ansley

Travels with my Rabbit

I was sitting on the lawn feeding my rabbit. Then I decided to get Nibbles out of his hutch. Suddenly he became a giant rabbit as if by magic. Then Nibbles spoke to me and said "I'm bored, can we go somewhere?"
"I know, why don't we go around the world?" I said.
"OK, but can we go with your friend Tansy and her rabbit Hazelnut?" asked Nibbs.
"Yeah, that's a brilliant idea." I reply.
"What are we waiting for?" we said. A few minutes later we arrived at Tansy's house.
"Hi," said Hazelnut.
"We are going to fly around the world. It will be amazing. Do you want to come with us?" We asked.
"Okay, we are up to a challenge," replied Tansy and Hazelnut.

We all decided to go to North Africa. We wanted to see lots of different animals but we only saw a beautiful tiger. I thought that the tiger was too scary so we decided to leave and go to Australia. In Australia we saw a graceful kangaroo.
"Hello" said Nibbs.

Danielle Bovis

My Hopes for the Future

I have one dream for the future, to grow up and be a fashion designer. When I was young I wanted to be a fashion designer, but wasn't quite sure what I would be doing. Would I be designing my own clothes and sending them off to be made by famous designers, or would I employ people to make them for me? If so, all the hard work I had put into designing the tops, hats, trousers or complete outfits would just go to waste.

So, when I got my present that I had longed for for my birthday, a design kit, I made a promise that I would make as many things as I could. Okay, maybe it was a miniature set and you made clothes for cardboard dolls who were about 9 inches tall, but at least it would help me on my way, wouldn't it? Then that same year, for Christmas I got a sewing box full of threads, needles, fabric and, most importantly, fabric glue and scissors. This may not seem like a lot to you, but it is to me. I'm not poor or anything, it was just that this would help me on my way as well.

Some of the designs I've made are things like Indian tops, trousers with tassels, boots with patterns and things. I don't really know any names of famous designers, but I know some clothes labels, such as Gucci and Sophie.

To this very day, I am still designing and making mini clothes.

Daydreaming

I was dreaming. Daydreaming of Gillingham, my favourite footie team. They needed to win the last match they played to come top of the league! As the match kicked off, I shot straight away... and I scored! Nasty Norwich City's ugly rubbish goalie picked the ball out of the net. Then, Great Gillingham's rubbish nutter of a left-back got himself sent off! And Nasty Norwich equalised from the subsequent penalty. One all. Nasty Norwich scored again, and again, and again; all from where Leon Johnsson (the left back) would have been if he wasn't sent off. Oh, I suppose the goals still would have gone in as he's not so much a left back as a drawback! But, anyway, at half time it was 7-1 to Nasty Norwich.

In the second half Nasty Norwich scored three more!   10-1 down. The commentary in the next five minutes went: "It's Boyns. GOAL! Kick off ... Boyns shoots. GOAL!" until it was nine goals to ten.

Just as we started to think we had a chance, the idiot between the sticks got sent off! But I wasn't finished. Oh no I wasn't! I picked it up, booted it and it went in! 10-10. In the last minute Great Gillingham got a penalty. I ran up, swung back and ...
"What are you doing? Do you know what we're talking about? " yelled Mr Hirons, my Maths teacher.
 Now I don't know if we won!

Joshua Cooper

The Rescuer

In one of my dreams, I am in my room at night and there is a fire
and I am the only one who wakes up. I tried to wake the others
up but they won't. So I got my mattress and threw it out the
window. Then I picked my Dad up and threw him on the
mattress, next my Mum, then my sister and my brother. I ran
down the stairs and got my dog and let her into the garden. Next,
I looked for my cats, but I could only find one of them. I began
to worry. I ran upstairs to look for her and I saw her in the
garden. I ran back to the stairs to find they have broken. I ran
down the hallway with the fire close behind and suddenly I
tripped over something, so I quickly got up and carried on. I saw
a window open in my brother's room so I ran and jumped out of
it. Luckily I landed on my Mum's car but I broke my leg. I
couldn't move and the fire got to the car and made the petrol
explode. I flew into the air and hit the wall and landed on the
floor. A tile hit me on the head and knocked me out and cut me
badly and I was pouring with blood. My family all woke up
because of the explosion and came and looked for me out the
front. The house slowly fell to the ground. They quickly put a T-
shirt on my head and got my next-door-neighbour. We got in her
car and went to the hospital. I could see myself lying in the bed
with my family around me but I never woke up.

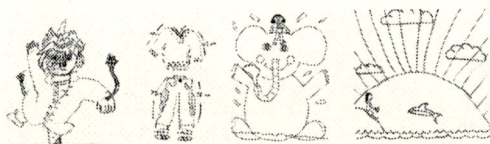

Joanne David

The Mermaid

I can remember one special dream I had when I was about six years old. During the day I had been to the seaside with my family and on the way back I fell asleep.

I dreamed that I was a mermaid. I had long hair and a funny fish tail, but I could still talk and act like a girl. I played with my friends under the water and we used to chase bubbles from the seaweed and play hide and seek in the rocks.

That day I was a mermaid and I went on a really exciting ride on the back of a seahorse. We saw lots of sharks and dolphins and big fish and I collected lots of shells. The seahorse took me back to my castle under the water and when Mum asked me if I had had a lovely time, I woke up and we were home.

I wish it had not been a dream.

Verity Dawkins

A Night in the Woods

I was having a sleepover with my friend Ellie and we were going on a bat hunt with my dogs called Flint and Abrik. We set off towards the lake, our spirits high and hoping that we would see the rare, large, horseshoe bat.

The moon was a tiny sliver in the sky and all we could hear was the crunch of the leaves beneath our feet. A sudden howl interrupted the silence. The dogs ran away, abandoning us in the cold and lonely forest. We called them back but they wouldn't come; they just kept on going. Ellie and I sat down, not knowing what to do; we had lost the dogs! Then a dog-like shape appeared, closely followed by six others. They were coming towards us.

"Flint, Abrik" I called, overjoyed they were back. A flash of lightning and I found out the truth. Their teeth were a little too long, their hair too short, and their eyes shone a little too brightly. They were not Flint and Abrik, they were wolves! And they were chasing after us!

"Run!" I screamed, but Ellie was already running. We ran through the woods but we were not fast enough, they were catching us up. I could hear the pad of their paws, their breath on my legs and their snouts a hair's breadth away from my ankles. We were going to be eaten alive! This was worse than my worst nightmare… and then I woke up!

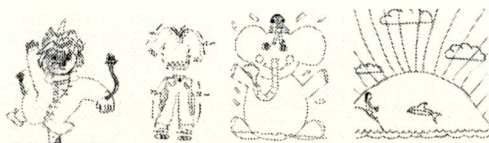

171

Daniel Gill

Escaping the Demons

Running as fast as I could away from what I thought could be my
death, I ran into a ghost train in the middle of the theme park.
Everybody had got away except me. I felt the hairs on the back
of my neck stand up, and then realised it wasn't such a good
hiding place from a demon that has horns and a long black cloak
that swishes in the air. I heard a grunt so I just jumped.

I was going to land on my feet but got swiped by a black Ferrari.
The driver looked in his twenties and my eyes turned to a piece
of card on the dashboard.
"Who are you?" I asked.
"I'll tell you when the moment is right," said the man.
"Well on this card it says you're I. C. Cruise."
"The moment has come - I am I .C. Cruise."
"Where are you taking me?"
"Away from these evil demons of hell."
Then, at around 120mph we turned a corner and saw at least one
hundred demons waiting to pounce. I.C. Cruise put his foot
down and blasted forward. The demons (not wanting to get run
down) parted and we went straight through the middle. Not
hesitating to look back, we went into a car park. I thought we had
lost them but no, they were closing in on us. Not knowing what
to do, I just ran! In a sweat I fell over. To my surprise the
demons got machine guns and started shooting at me. Then I
woke up. I was confused. My Mum called me downstairs for
breakfast. Then I realised it was a dream.

172

Katie Golding

My Hope For The Future

My hope for the future is to swim with dolphins. I have wanted to do this for years and years. It all started when I was watching the TV when I was seven or eight years old and I saw some people swimming with dolphins. As soon as I saw them I knew that that was what I wanted to do the most. I want to do this because I would like to feel what the dolphins are like and play with them, and have that wonderful experience of being with them and having a good time.

If and when I get to do my dream I hope that the dolphins will feel smooth and soft, that they will be nice and play with me, and that they will talk and maybe do some tricks too.

The tricks I hope that they will do are jumping through hoops and maybe having a person standing one foot on each dolphin and watch them go sort of water-skiing on dolphins I suppose. They might even let me hold onto one of the dolphin's fins whilst the dolphins swim. They might also do a trick where they put something like a plant pot in a wooden box and fill it with water. Then they hold up two objects, one of which is the correct one, and the dolphins will just know which one is the right object.

This is my dream because I think that I will enjoy it very much and that it will also be a fantastic experience. I also want to do this so that I can see them do their fantastic tricks.

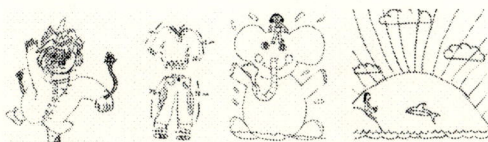

Alice Gouldsworthy

The Blue Monkey

A gigantic dinosaur was walking past our house. It was the most terrifying thing I had seen in my whole life. Then I remembered it was Sid, my friend the dinosaur I met in my last dream. He told me about the blue monkey in Africa. He said "You have to save it before Kitty (the most evil person in the world) does to save our world."
"OK, I'll see what I can do." I replied.

We went to Africa and it took us half a second to get there. He showed me this peculiar tree that has different-coloured leaves - purple, yellow, grey, pink, blue, green, brown and all the colours you could think of. Then suddenly the highest, most beautiful gold leaf spoke to me, "Why are you here?" said the leaf.
"I..I..I've come to s-see th-the person who owns the blue m-mon-n-key." I hesitated.
Suddenly, as quick as a flash, arrows and swords were flying everywhere. "You can't escape now," cackled the leaf.

After weeks, we were still not out. By this time our tummies were rumbling, roaring with hunger. We couldn't take it any more. After four months with no food, no water, we were released. "Promise you won't look for the blue monkey," ordered the leaf, "or you will be locked up for ever." Sid and I walked on and found a stall and saw the blue monkey. Suddenly I woke up. I couldn't believe it was a dream, then I looked outside and saw the blue monkey in the tree.

174

Judd Gurr

T-Rex Nightmare

It may have been the scariest dream ever, or was it real? What had happened? Was it a dream or not? It started before the nightmare. I got a drink, put it in my room and then I went to sleep.

I woke up and heard a sound outside. I looked at my drink. It was moving and the water was going from side to side. I walked up to the window slowly. The noise had stopped outside the next window. I was scared. I went to the next window, but the noise had moved back. I was now very scared. I ran back, then opened the curtains and there in front of me was a T-Rex's golden eyes looking through the window at me. I froze, then it roared and then I fainted.

I woke up in the morning. I had a nose bleed and I was on the floor and the window was open and the curtains were open too. It felt so real. I had been on my bed but now I was on the floor next to the window. Was it a nightmare or was it a dream?

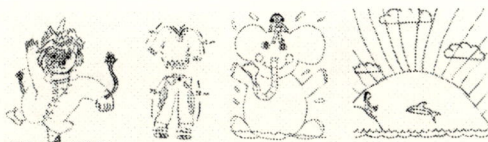

Luke Hagreen

The Day I Had Been Waiting For

Early one morning my Mum woke me up and said that I had a
visitor, so I put my dressing gown on and went downstairs and
saw Alex Ferguson. I rubbed my eyes with amazement.
"What are you doing here? Haven't you got the FA Cup Final
today against Arsenal?"
"Yes, but there's a problem, Van Nistelrooy has dropped out and
I wanted to know whether you can fill his position."

5.45pm
"Come on lads, this is the big day. The FA cup final against
Arsenal." Roy Keane said in a competitive voice. Suddenly the
manager came in to tell us the formation.
"OK, this is the formation. Carroll in goal, Hebnize left back,
O'Shea then Ferdinand, also G Neville at right back. In midfield
we have Giggs on the left, centre left is Keane, centre right is
Scholes and on the right is Ronaldo. Up front on left is Rooney
and on the right wearing number 15 is the young man himself,
it's Luke Hagreen!"
"Yyyyeeeaaaarrr!" roared the crowd as the players came out.

We were off to a bad start. Henry scored for Arsenal but then
Rooney scored. At half time the score was 1-1. In the second half
we got another goal, which was scored by me, Luke Hagreen,
meaning the final score was 2-1 to us.
At that point I woke up and realised it was just a dream.

"You're Under Arrest "

It all started when my Mum and I were out riding together and talking about what job I wanted when I was older. I said that I wanted to join the mounted police. Then she went on and on saying that I had to join the police and go in for the mounted later. I told her that I knew all that but she still went on. Finally I squeezed my legs and asked Pepi to trot on to get away from all that noise.

When I got home I tied Pepi up and took off his bridle and saddle, then quickly got his rug and walked him to the field. When I was going down there, I was thinking about how I would get into the police. Then I came out of my daydream and realised that I was on the floor. Pepi was eating the beautiful green grass that we were supposed to save for the winter but, as Pepi was such a pig, he had eaten nearly all of it. I quickly got up, caught him and put him out in the bottom field. Then I took all of my stuff to the house and went up to my room and lay on my bed. I got up a few minutes later and went outside. There I saw three big bays about 16.3hh. They were all geldings. I looked up and saw one man and two women. One said to me, "I heard that you want to join the police."
I said, "Yes, who told you?"
"Never you mind. Well, I have talked to the Chief and the Ma'am and they have given you a place in the force."
"But don't you have to go in for training?"

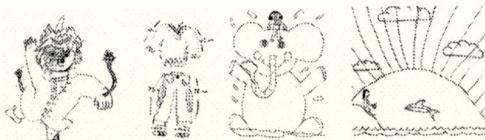

James Hill

The James Sheep

On the first Saturday in May a lady came to shear our fifty sheep. She got out her shearing gear and began. My brother George was helping her, but I was in bed. I had just come out of my bedroom and was looking over the fence, watching them. I felt so tired because I had been to a concert and had not got back until one o'clock in the morning.

"Look!" cried Dad. "Look at that sheep, it looks just like James."
"Yeh," I replied. "Me with white hair."

A couple of minutes later I went back to bed because I was so tired. I lay on my bed and closed my eyes. A few minutes later, to my utter astonishment, I had turned into a sheep.

I went downstairs and tried to tell my Dad, but he did not seem to see or hear me. I yelled, but the only noise I could make was baa, baa. I went into the field and saw lots of other sheep. When they saw me they began to sing.

"Baa baa white sheep, have you any wool?
Yes sir, yes sir, fifty bags full.
One for Miss Christmas and one for Mr Hill
and the others we will sell at the market place."

Suddenly I was grabbed, made to swim through the horrible greasy dip and then to my horror, I realised I was going to be shorn. At last it was finished and I was very glad. Then I awoke with a jump, and realised I had been dreaming.

Marcus Hood

Zombie Dreams

The most exciting dream I ever had was when a zombie rose from the dead in Boughton Monchelsea. The zombie was killing lots of people and turned them into zombies too. John and I jumped into a DB9 and Matthew and Dan had somehow got hold of an AM Vanquish and they had caught up with us by the time we had got to the M20. Then we found out that the zombies had got a Lamborghini Diablo. "We are going to have to drive very quickly to beat that," I said.

Then John, Matthew, Dan, me and the zombies found guns and a lifetime's worth of ammo and I said that we could use this. We started shouting at the zombies, shouting
"Ha, ha, ha, ha, ha."
By then our grip on our tyres was bare and our fuel was low too. We did a pit stop in a Shell Garage. It took ten seconds. For the zombies it took fifteen seconds because one of the zombie's arms fell off. We were on the M20 and we could see a roundabout. We went round but the zombies shot one of the back tyres so we skidded and crashed!
Then I woke up.

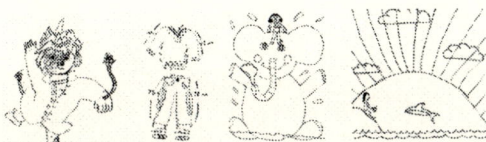

Amy Horton

The Dream of Africa

My lifelong dream would be to go to Africa and hold a tiger. So
this is how it goes. I went in for a competition to go to Africa
and help feed the tigers. Then one day I got a letter telling me I
had won it and oh, just to let you know, it was for the person
who knew the most about tigers. So I went to show Mum and
she was so glad I had won it. Ben came down to ask what was
wrong and Mum told him. He jumped up and down, really
excited, but then I told him that there were only two people
allowed but then I said he could save up.

It's been a week and Ben was able to save up. We are now on the
plane. Oh, you might think it's a bit cruel for Ben to pay for his
own ticket but it's my dream! Then the ride seems really short so
we get off the plane and there's someone waiting for us, so we
get in the car and drive to the tiger park. When we get there I go
first and see all the tigers. Secondly I watch them get their food.
So then I'll have a go at feeding them. Thirdly I go into a tiger
cage with baby tigers and they like me so much I am allowed to
have one and I call it Songa. On the way back to the hotel, Ben is
messing around and Songa doesn't like it so he bites Ben and
makes him bleed a bit.

When we get to the hotel, Songa and I get a room to ourselves.

Sam Howell

The Leader of the Wolves

This is a weird nightmare.

"What? I have to go to bed, but it's still light!" I shouted in an angry voice. I ran upstairs and fell asleep. I didn't know I was asleep. It all seemed real. I was standing in the middle of the forest running for my life. I saw a light, then I was getting surrounded with wolves and I screamed.

"What are you doing?" said the wolves.

I was confused, the wolves looked hungry, so I said, "Please don't hurt me, I won't hurt you" .

"Don't worry, our leader will deal with you," said the wolves.

"Hi" said the glow. Suddenly it was, it was...

"Thierry Henry - what...?" I was gobsmacked.

"Yes, I am Henry, don't wear me out" said Henry.

"What do you want? Your wolves said you'll deal with me" I said.

"Well, I will deal with you," said Henry. Suddenly he disappeared and I ran to the glow. I wasn't sure what it was so I walked into it.

I was travelling through lights and ended up in a tunnel. It wasn't a car tunnel, it was a football tunnel. Then a man asked me what the password was and I heard a whisper, it was Henry and he said "Vavavoom." "Vavavoom." I said and we walked onto the pitch. We had just kicked off and I had the ball and shot. Someone had fouled me. It was a penalty. I was so nervous but I had a shot - and scored. Suddenly I saw flashing lights and woke up in my football boots.

Kerry Jones

Volcano Disaster

I was living in 72 Winlaton Road, but it was no ordinary road. There was a volcano at the end of it!! One day my Mum and I were shopping at the Co-op and we had just finished packing when suddenly we heard an alarm. It was not an ordinary alarm, but it was the eruption alarm! We headed home and when we got there we found all of our family were there.

Anyway, there was a massive earthquake, then suddenly a huge jet of boiling hot lava came out of the ground, but as quick as it had come, the jet disappeared, leaving a huge hole in the middle of the garden. We all thought nothing else out of the ordinary would happen, and then a little green lady came out of the hole! She was wearing a black dress with a black shawl over the top and a black pointy hat. A second after she appeared she turned into a bright green dragon and I screamed and woke up…

I was in a zoo with a friend and there were loads of animals going past. I tried to stroke a rabbit but when I reached out all I felt was cold glass - we were in a glass box! Three wolves came up to the glass and stood on their hind legs and got one of their claws and started to make a very big rectangle! When they had finished, they took the glass away. Suddenly they turned on me growling, and my friend turned to me and said, "I am sorry Kerry, but they are hungry and need some food."
They leapt at me and I thought I was going to be eaten alive and then again, I woke up.

David Kenward

Helping Sharks

When I have nightmares it makes me in a bad mood the next day, so how I clear my brain is to think of sharks. Bull and Wobbegong Shark and their families were dying of pollution. I wanted to help them by cleaning the bottom of the sea from the dirt which nasty men put there. I had this digger which can be attached to a boat and the back hose can go to the very bottom of the sea and dig it up.

There was this policeman who was crossing the ocean in an aircraft carrier, which had cans full of oil to use on the machinery. He threw an empty one overboard, which I saw as I was under the water in my diving suit with an air tank on my back. It hit my friend the Wobbegong shark on the tail, which wounded him. I went down to the seabed where he was lying and saw blood on his tail. The next thing I heard was a strange wailing noise which was coming from a hammerhead shark who had smelt the blood and was heading towards my friend. I took my waterproof pistol and fired three shots near his head to frighten him away, which it did. I swam ashore to get my waterproof bandages and came back to him, but he wasn't there!! I searched for him and found him in a net. Luckily I had my scissors so I cut him free and bandaged him up.

I tied a special rope round his belly and towed him through the water, carried him home with me and put him into the bath and ran the water.

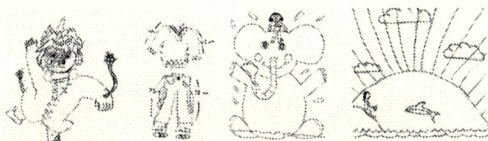

Jessica Kilbride

Aliens, Pegs and Paper Knives

It was an ordinary night and I had just got into bed and closed my eyes. I suddenly felt like I was falling. I opened my eyes and looked at my clock. It said 8:00am. I got out of bed and went down for breakfast, but Mum and Dad weren't there. I went into the kitchen and looked out of the front window, and there, pegged on our washing line, were my parents' clothes but the scary thing was my parents were still in them. This sort of thing doesn't happen every day! I ran outside and unpegged them. Then I noticed everyone else was pegged up too. So me, Mum and Dad unpegged as many as we could.
"What happened?" I asked.
"Well," said Mum. "Aliens landed their spaceship on the school and have been attacking people with pegs."
Suddenly a green blobby thing slithered past, it was disgusting.
"Are they aliens?" I asked. "Yes," everyone replied.
"I have a plan," I said. "Right, get a paper knife everyone. We are going to kill the aliens with paper knives."
So we went to where the aliens had landed their spaceship.

Suddenly thousands and thousands of slime green blobby things filed out of the spaceship. Soon we found ourselves face to face with them. We were just about to attack when a little boy ran out of the crowd shouting, "Please go away aliens, please, please."
"OK," they said and they all went back to the spaceship and left. I tripped over and banged my head. Everything went black.
"Wake up," said Mum. I was back in my bed!

184

Rhiannon King

They're Not Dolphins, They're SHARKS

I was sailing the bright blue Mediterranean to search for an injured dolphin. The sun was at its brightest. Just putting on my suit, I noticed something in the water, but I completely ignored it and dived in. The cold water shocked me like a freezing cold drink. It was beautiful down here. I swam deeper and deeper. It got more lovely every minute. The sea was ever so clear. I could see miles ahead of me, the plants were swaying to and fro with the current. Fish swam in and out of them, swimming right past me.

That's when I saw a dolphin. She was gorgeous but the poor thing, she was stuck and very badly injured. Then I spotted what looked like more dolphins. I swam closer. They swam closer. Forgetting about the injured dolphin I swam up to stroke the rest of the group… suddenly I discovered that they were really sharks!!!

The sharks were coming closer. Thrashing their tails, the sharks' beady eyes were gleaming as red as rubies, their jaws wide open showing me their frightening knife-like teeth.

They were gaining on me! They tried to attack me! I swam as fast as I could but I was too slow, too late, I was, I was…

Then I woke up.

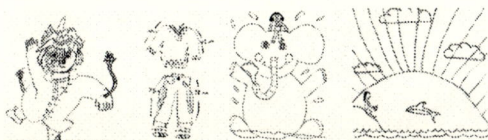

Gabriella Knowler

The Big Jump

In the future I hope I will be able to bungee jump. One night I dreamt that I did it and this is what happened.

As I went to the edge of the platform my stomach started churning as I got ready to jump. I looked down and saw what seemed like a cavern one hundred miles deep. My insides felt like they were doing aerobatics as I stepped forward and bent my wobbly knees and... jumped!

I saw the ground start rushing towards me, everything started to get closer and closer as I got frightening thoughts like "what if the rope broke?" and "what if it stretched too far and I crashed?" Then I forgot about all the horrid possibilities and I realised that the rope had stopped stretching and I was just about to go flying towards the sky. The thoughts came to me again and again as I went up and down, up and down. Minutes later, after all the bouncing, someone grabbed me by the waist and pulled me up.

As I put my feet onto the platform, I stood up with legs made of jelly and I was shaking. As I went and walked back, I found it difficult to walk in a straight line. My family looked up as I went down the ladder and tried to climb down and reach the ground again. Many thoughts ran through my head about whether I should ever try and do it again.

Only in my wildest dreams!

Colleen McGivern

The Sandy Dream

I was lying on the sandy beach and the sun was beating down on the ground. Suddenly something hit me on the toes of my foot. I found that it was a black shell. I rubbed off all the sand and as I did so I found that there was someone or other talking to me. I listened and realised it was a dolphin.

"Hey you!" the dolphin said, "My name is Sandy. Would you like to come and ride on my back?"

"Yes please!" I yelled eagerly. "My name is Ellie."

Having decided to go onto the dolphin's back, I found myself running out to Sandy. We went surprisingly deep under the water. Sandy was giving me an underwater tour of the sea that he knew. He did quite a few tricks, but I fell off his back on one of them. I tried to talk but found that I couldn't.

"Ellie" he said, sounding worried. "Can you swim over to me?"

I nodded and started swimming, then I jumped onto his back.

"Why couldn't I breathe?" I asked curiously.

"Well, you have to be on my back otherwise you aren't be able to breathe!" Sandy said.

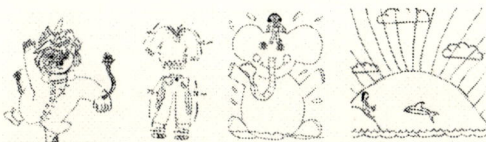

Jurassic Dreams

Early one morning I woke up on my sofa. I thought it was a
normal day and got up. I had been begging my Mum to go to
Jurassic Park Junior Camp all the previous day. I went into the
kitchen and my Mum was there making breakfast. She said,
"Come on, hurry up, you don't want to be late for Jurassic Park
Junior Camp." She meant it!

The car journey felt like it took forever. I said, "The only way
there is by helicopter," so she dropped me off and we went. The
helicopter journey only took ten minutes and we were there, in
paradise. THE JURASSIC PARK! So we went to the camp
admiring all the dinosaurs on the way. I saw a particularly funny
dinosaur called Bronkosaurus. We heard all the rules. Then we
heard an ererrrrrr - the security fence had broken down and the
T-rex and all the other dinosaurs got loose, then a tiny dinosaur
snuck in and sprayed one of the kids. Luckily we had a first aid
kit so he was OK. Everyone was scared.

Thud! …. thud!! …. THUD!!! …. It went silent and then we
heard a roar. Everyone hid, but I didn't, I just stood there. A
woman ran up to me and put this smelly stuff on my face and
then the roof flew open and a boy screamed in horror as the
T-rex roared and ran off. We all ran and got in the helicopter.
We got well away for now. Ahhhh! Huh, what happened, where
am I? I got up and went to the dining room and my Mum was
normal - it was a dream. Oh well, it was fun anyway.

188

Dolphin Diving

It is 8 o'clock at night and I am just about to go to bed. I got up
onto my bed and shut my eyes. Just then I felt myself fall. I woke
up, got out of my bed and looked at the clock. Three o'clock in
the morning, how strange. I only just went to bed. I chucked on
my clothes, went outside and found myself in Florida. There
were millions of people queuing outside my house.
"What are you doing outside my house?"
"Well, if you hadn't noticed, you're right outside the dolphin
court." Said a man near my front door.
"What do you mean?"
"You're right outside the dolphin court, that's what I mean."

I went inside, put on my cossy and went back outside to join the
queue. Three hours later I was going to be next to swim with the
dolphins. Yes, yes, yes!!!
"What is the matter?" Said a man in front of me. Yes this is it. I
was going in the gates.
"Three pounds please. If you go down the steps the lady will
show you which dolphins you will be riding."
"Oh, thank you!"

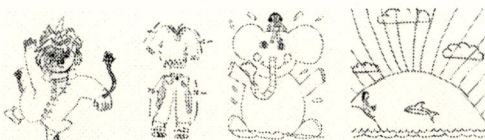

Ashley Ribbands

Movie Dreams – an extract

Did you know, some dreams you have will be from a movie, e.g. Metropolis. This is the first scene of one my dreams.

A mysterious man came to a laboratory. He said a password (in Chinese). The door opened and there was a giant container with a window in it. Inside the container was a girl with lots of hair on her head. The man touched the window. He said, "It's beautiful." He shed a tear and it landed on his arm and sparkled like a diamond. The man walked back to the door. One of her eyes opened. Her scanner pointed to the man. She said "Father," then she was shocked. The door closed and she said "Don't leave me here." She shed a tear and tried to get this metal plate off her waist. I came in unexpectedly and I broke the computer (the password one). The door opened, I broke her out. We ran out. Secretly a boy with sunglasses, gelled hair and a pistol spied on us. He mumbled, "She should not be on the throne, my father should."

I spotted my Grandpa eating a hotdog at a burger stand on Robo Street, Metropolis, Japan.
"Grandpa, Grandpa, I found a girl with fatal injuries." I shouted.
"She is a replica of … oh my!" said Grandpa.
"What?" I asked.
"The President's daughter," he explained. "Ten years ago the President of Metropolis had a daughter. The girl ran away. She is going to destroy Metropolis."

190

John Sharp

A Dream Come True

So here I am wanting to be a footballer. Mum came in and said,
"What is the matter?"
"I want to be a footballer!"
"Well go and be one then, what team?"
"Man U."
"Oh, that's good. I've got Alex Ferguson's phone number here."
So the next day I ring him up. He tells me he's got one space left
in his team and asks me to come over at lunchtime the next day.
"You're one minute late!" He says when I arrive, "Here's your
shirt, it's number 12."
"Yes, I've always wanted to be that number," I reply.
"Well come on then, hurry up, run around the pitch three times."
says Alex Ferguson. Okay, 1,2,3, laps done. "Okay, you can go
home now, John."
"See you tomorrow."
"I'm home Mum, where's my dinner?" I ask as I walk through
the door.
"In the oven"
"Cheers. This is the best dinner ever."
That's how I dreamed of becoming a footballer.

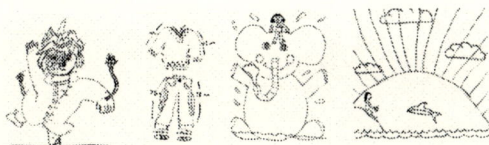

Jump!

I was in an aeroplane. A big man came over to me. On his shirt
he had a badge saying Dave. So I said "Hello Dave, why am I on
this aeroplane again?"
"Remember, you're going to jump with a parachute, of course,
for charity".
"What am I going to do?" I whispered to myself.
"Come on," said Dave.
"Am I jumping yet?" I asked.
"No, in a minute." He said.
"What then?" I said with relief.
"Get into the changing room and put this suit on," he said. So I
went into the changing room and got the suit on. It was
waterproof. It was like a top and trousers in one and you zip it up
at the back. It was horrible but the colour was nice - it was pink,
powder pink.
"Sorry, but I didn't know it was going to be powder pink!" Dave
said, laughing.
"It's not funny!" I shouted.
"It's nearly time," he shouted as he opened the door. The wind
came rushing in so hard it blew me over.
I walked to the edge of the plane and said "I'll get this over and
done with." I took a deep breath and jumped! I screamed as I
fell.
"I forgot my parachute!" I screamed. I saw the ground and
suddenly I bounced up - I was on a trampoline. Then I woke up
and saw a toy aeroplane. It was all a dream.

Michael Stringer

Teachers' Wars

The best dream I had was what I called "Teachers' Wars". It started like an ordinary day. When I woke up I was in Jedi clothes with a belt holding a light sabre. Then I knew I had powers. I tried to use the force to get out my light sabre. At first I couldn't so I tried again, and finally got it out and put it back in. Then the windows smashed. I got out my light sabre. It was very tense. My senses were strong. Someone was going to smash through the roof. Just then the roof was broken by some lightning.

I found myself in a circle of evil Jedi teachers. One of them was the leader, Daft Taylor. Then through the door came Master Yoda. One of the teachers went to fight me. We fought for two hours. Then Daft Taylor came after me. I just kept fighting. I kept on stabbing him, but he wouldn't die. An old teacher came and said "Pie." I just said "What?" "Pie, you said pie." "No, I said die." Daft Taylor went for me again, but then I jumped behind him and …

I was awake for real (I thought) but I noticed I was still in my robes and my light sabre. I was still in my dream… arrrrrgggghhhh.

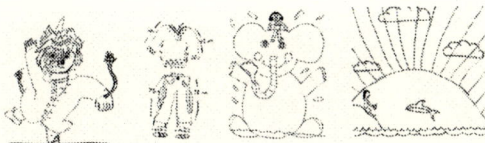

Tansy Tester

Me And Norbert

It all started when I was arguing with my Mum about me wanting to go to Africa and seeing my favourite animal, elephants.
"We haven't got the money," she said.
"That's unfair," I said and stomped off into my room.
I laid on my bed thinking about how great it would be to ride an elephant.

A few minutes later I got up and went outside into the garden. I couldn't believe it, I was in Africa. The beautiful beaming sun was shining down on me and there was a lovely lake with elephants bathing in the cool water. I ran over to them. They were so friendly. I would have thought they would stomp away, but they didn't. They splashed me with water and I had ever so much fun. I went back into the house dripping wet and told my Mum how much fun I had with the elephants. I put some dry clothes on and my Mum said that I was allowed to ride an elephant. I ran back outside and my Mum helped me on to the biggest elephant. His name was Norbert and he looked so beautiful. We were in the woods and Norbert said to me,
"Do you want to go to a much more exciting place than this?"
"You can talk!" I said.
"Yep." Said Norbert.
Suddenly Norbert started to fly.
"Where are we going?" I asked.
"Elephant land," he replied.

Megan Underdown

Donays Peak

Be warned, this is no ordinary story... As we were coming back
from Nanny's house, Mum said that I should get some rest
because it was past nine and that's when I go to bed. So I did.
It was a very short sleep and when I woke up I saw a horseman -
half man, half human. By that time everyone looked like him
except Mum, Dad and I. It looked more like daylight than night
time. Also I thought we were meant to go home instead of going
to something called Donays Peak... A strange man took us inside
and shut the steel gate behind us.

We walked a bit further and saw a play area. As we went in we
heard a slam and a zip sound and we found the play area was an
hallucination - there were sharks swimming about in some water,
and the only way to get out was to step on some pads in front of
us. Just then we thought of turning back but there was a steel
gate that had shut after us again. We went further in and saw a
man struggling for help. Strangely enough he wasn't a horseman,
he was a normal person. We tried to pull him out but then he
disappeared underwater. The sharks were pushing the pads and
Dad nearly fell. It seemed like the torture would never end.

I blinked and then I was in my car again. It was like it had
happened all by magic...

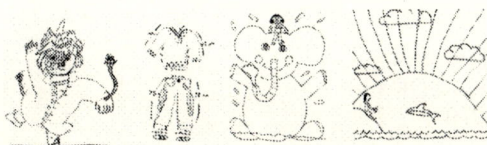

Printed in the United Kingdom
by Lightning Source UK Ltd.
104860UKS00001B/133-291

9 781845 490287